Shaping Your Future through
Imagination and Design

J. Gerald Suárez, Ph.D.

ISBN: 13: 9781494401368

ISBN: 10: 1494401363

Library of Congress Control Number: 2013923456
CreateSpace Independent Publishing Platform
North Charleston, South Carolina

To my mother, who gave me the foundation for a bright future

To my family, who continually give me a great present

Contents

Acknowledgments

It has been my dream to write a book that reflects my philosophy and experiences in the White House, the boardroom, and the classroom and to pay tribute to the major influences in my thinking. They include the following individuals:

My mentor, Dr. Russell L. Ackoff, with whom I collaborated for sixteen years. Russ's wisdom influenced my life like no other, and his friendship and good memories forever live in my heart.

Dr. W. Edwards Deming, with whom I learned so much and filmed the Better Management for a Changing World series, "Managing Fear in the Workplace."

Dr. Stephen R. Covey, whose example and work have had an enduring impact on my life and the lessons I put forth in the book.

Joel A. Barker, who helped me appreciate the power of vision and the tools to get to the future faster.

I also learned invaluable leadership lessons from President Bill Clinton, for whom I had the honor to work and travel with for eight years, and President George W. Bush, with whom I worked for over three years, which included the tragic events of September 11 as well as the wars in Iraq and Afghanistan.

I'm indebted to Allie Armitage and Bobbie Ryan for their relentless encouragement, support, and assistance throughout this project. Their passion and commitment were instrumental in making this book a reality. A special thanks to my friend and colleague, Dr. Rob Sheehan, for his unwavering support.

A word of gratitude goes to all the participants in my executive sessions as well as my students and colleagues, in particular those whom I talk about in this book. I owe them much for having the resiliency to become Leaders of One and the courage to shape the future.

Finally, to my wife and children—their unconditional love fueled my inspiration and lifted me up when I needed it the most.

To all of you, thank you!

Preface

Nobody gets to write your destiny but you. Your future is in your hands. Your life is what you make of it, and nothing—absolutely nothing—is beyond your reach so long as you're willing to dream big, so long as you're willing to work hard.

—President Barack Obama, Julia Masterman High School, Philadelphia, September 14, 2010

These are inspiring words. Why, then, is shaping the future so hard to do? Too often, life gets in the way. We drift away from whatever we feel passionate about, driven by the demands of making a living or getting ready to make a living. These practicalities eventually take precedence. We may say:

"I can't afford to stop what I'm doing now. I need to get established first."

"I need to graduate, and then I'll think about my future."

"I'm unemployed. The last thing I can afford to do is dream."

"I feel I've missed my calling, but I can't afford to go back now and start again."

"I'm not in charge."

"I can't think about the future. I have pressing problems today."

"I can't stop to think about innovation. I have pressing operational priorities."

When we don't give ourselves the time to reflect upon how we are leading our future, we fail to leverage our potential.

Imagine asking an architect to design a house for you, yet you do not offer any information about what kind of house you want, who is going to live in it, how much money you have for it, and so forth. It would be impossible to design and worse yet to build. The same can happen if you think of your future without asking yourself some key questions. Consider your answers to the following questions:

"What am I most passionate about?"

"What do I value?"

"What am I most proud of?"

"If I could create a new present for myself right now, what would it look like?"

Stephen Covey, author of *The 7 Habits of Highly Effective People,* reminds us that "all things are created twice; there is a first or mental creation, and then there is a second or physical creation."[1] Anything that's new is conceived first in thought. Dreaming is the mental creation; design, the explicit manifestation of those dreams into something real.

Everything around us is the byproduct of dream and design—bridges, buildings, airplanes, networks, furniture, clothing. All went through the same process. We have no problem understanding how design works in the creation of a physical object but do not understand how it can work to shape our future.

What makes the task of envisioning and creating a desirable future so difficult is the gap we impose between our thoughts and our actions. T. S. Eliot, probably the most influential poet of the twentieth century, describes the dilemma in *The Hollow Men*: "Between the conception and the creation, Between the emotion and the response, Falls the shadow."[2]

The gap in time and space between what we desire and what it takes to achieve it is often filled with fear, uncertainty, worry, conflicting priorities, and real and self-imposed obstructions. We create barriers to change, because to shape our future, to take control of it, means to take on activities that require purposeful action. Transformations of any kind are not easy because they require us do two of the toughest things in life: to start something new and to stop something old.

It is here that too often we invent our best excuses, abandon our professional aspirations, and postpone our personal desires. But if we choose, instead, to take actions that connect us to what we most desire, we can create a future for ourselves that has meaning and impact.

Complete the following sentences:

"I am most energized when..."

"I have always dreamed of..."

"I derive joy from..."

If there is a disconnect between how you completed these statements and your present reality, something is getting in the way.

Most of us want to do better. We like to believe in a place called "tomorrow," and at the most visceral level we want tomorrow to be better than today. Our ability to imagine the future is what separates us from all other animals.

We go to school because we want to learn and progress. We work hard not just to provide the basics but also to increase our standard of living. We try to eat well and exercise because we believe we can extend our quality of life, now and in the future.

The hope for a better future is universal. Along the way, however, it's easy to lose our sense of hope and optimism. We confuse means with ends, activity with progress, efficiency with effectiveness, and busyness with importance, and we end up in what Stephen Covey calls the "thick of thin things," trapped in the tyranny of the present.

I have learned about these impediments to action in my role as an educator and consultant. In my job as a consultant, I help corporations and government agencies envision an ideal future for their organizations and to systematically work back to the present to create the conditions to make it happen. It's a process rooted in systems thinking called *idealized design.*[3] I was lucky enough to learn how it works firsthand from one of the most brilliant systems thinkers of the twentieth century, Russell Ackoff. To me, Russ was a friend and mentor. To the world, he was a renowned professor emeritus from the University of Pennsylvania's Wharton School of Business, a prolific writer, and a pragmatic philosopher. Regrettably, he died in 2009, but his legacy lives on.

Russ taught me that what happens between the present and the future mostly depends on our actions. We can shape our future, but doing so requires leadership. It takes courage. The trappings of the present too often interfere with our capacity to dream of and design a better future. How then to overcome these obstructions?

The methodology is simple, yet the implications are profound. I describe a cycle of activities that begins with the mental creation of an idealized future and ends with its realization. These four phases—Contemplation, Desire, Design, and Creation—work together in a holistic fashion. This book is organized to help you follow the process in a sequential flow. The Contemplation-Desire-Design-Creation (CDDC) cycle is a powerful and transformative methodology that will unleash you from the present and allow you to interact with the future that you want to create.

This book acknowledges leadership as a dynamic process of influence and creation. It aims to help you awaken the leader in yourself. The book has personal and organizational leadership applications. In fact, this distinction will be blurred. As Gandhi noted, "One man cannot do right in one department of life whilst he is occupied in doing wrong in any other department. Life is one indivisible whole." [4] Similarly, leadership is one indivisible whole.

This book offers a way to help you transcend the present—its trappings and obstacles—and create for yourself and others a viable and vibrant future. The book is filled with stories to inspire as well as exercises and tools to help you lead your own way and "write your destiny."

As Benjamin Mays said, "The tragedy of life doesn't lie in not reaching your goal. The tragedy lies in having no goal to reach. It isn't a calamity to die with dreams unfulfilled, but it is a calamity not to dream. It is no disgrace to reach for the stars and come up short, but it is a disgrace not to have stars to reach for. Not failure, but low aim, is a sin." [5]

Becoming a "Leader of One" and taking on the challenge of shaping your future is not easy. Transformative efforts never are. The task ahead will feel overwhelming, but commitment to initiate and sustain action, no matter how small, will move you closer to a new and desired reality.

There are no shortcuts. Every building begins its climb upward with a single brick, every marathon race with a single step, and every book with a single word. The same can be said for every minute of your life, so seconds count. The first steps are always the most difficult, but each one will bring you closer to "there."

Washington, DC   J. Gerald Suárez
May 2014

Introduction

Do not follow where the path may lead; go instead where there is no path and leave a trail.

—Ralph Waldo Emerson, American Lecturer, Essayist, and Poet

I employ idealized design methodology not only in the boardroom but also in the classroom. I teach at the University of Maryland Robert H. Smith School of Business. The courses and custom seminars focus on leadership, quality management, systems thinking, innovation, organizational design, and strategy. For me, it's heady stuff.

I place emphasis on learning by doing. In one of my courses, I ask students to propose and carry out project ideas to which they have a personal connection and where the outcome will have a positive consequence for society as a whole. The students use the methodologies espoused in this book, and the impact is remarkable.

In preparing the students for their work, I throw out questions that ask them to "dig deep" for answers, questions similar to those mentioned in the Preface. Their responses have been extraordinary. Very seldom, if ever, has anyone asked them to design their dream job or their ideal future or to articulate their aim. It is the essential first step in this revolutionary transition process, critical to organizational redesign and critical to reshaping your future. The late Russell Ackoff explained it best: "Idealized design is a way of thinking about change that is deceptively simple to state: In solving problems of virtually any kind, the way to get the best outcome is to imagine what the ideal solution would be and then work backward to where you are today. This ensures that you do not erect imaginary obstacles before you even know what the ideal is."[1] It saves you from yourself as you work from B to A.

I usually begin the first day of a new session by asking students why they are there. Participants have told me that their colleagues recommended my courses because they offered leadership lessons that could be applied to life as a whole, not just to organizations. They heard about the stories and the methodologies that were part of the class and how those made the course practical, relevant, and inspiring. The approach could help them shape a better future, in both their personal and professional lives.

Eventually, students and clients alike began to urge me to write a book about what they were learning. We were all of a mind that shaping the future did not require holding a position of power. The power comes from within.

As I began to write, I realized that the personal stories of my students, clients, and colleagues echoed in my mind. They all had dreams for themselves that had gone unfulfilled. They hoped for a better future or a better job, but they didn't know how to achieve it. Since my work with idealized design began, a number of them have taken action and are now succeeding as they move in new directions.

How to capture those stories in a way that would make sense to others? My schedule was tight, and there was no time to write a book. I began by writing it on the fly, literally—in the air, on the ground, standing up, sitting down. I structured these reflections into a cohesive whole. The book that emerged is a synthesis of experiential insight, inspiring stories, practical tools, and sound theory to take you through four stages of transformative action and guide you in becoming a Leader of One.

You have the power to shape your future if you are willing to find and unleash the leader within. It begins with determining what truly inspires you. You can find inspiration in many sources, but I contend that probably the most important source is deep within, waiting to be uncovered and nurtured. When you are asked, for example, what work you would do for free, you are forced to think of the experiences that have been the most memorable, the most rewarding, and the most inspiring.

The word inspiration comes from the old French word *inspirer* and the Latin *inspirare*, which means "to breathe into, to inhale." [2] Inspiration is a creative, positive force. To breathe is to live. Breathing is essential for life, and inspiration is equally essential for living a life of meaning and consequence. My ultimate goal is for the readers to "breathe in" the possibilities, and "breathe out" the leadership actions that have enduring impact in the workplace, in their lives, and in the lives of others.

I emphasize throughout the book how we are all connected to one another. John Donne tells us that "no man is an island."[3] Our behaviors have consequences for those around us. Whatever we wish for, it cannot come at their expense. Our aspirations must take the dreams of others into account and must always remain within the healthy context of a cherished and shared ambition.

I emphasize how in the scale of life, we must seek a balance. We should not take away more than we are willing to put in as we shape our future. If the scale is out of balance, it should be tilted toward giving, not getting. In *Your Money or Your Life*, authors Vicki Robin and Joe Dominguez talk about the need to change the way we relate to money so that we can live a more purposeful life and experience a sense of well-being. "Beyond the point of enough, we achieve happiness by exercising our capacity to give."[4]

Shaping the future is hard work because it requires that we change our thinking and behavior in important ways. Think of an old habit that you would like to kick—why do you procrastinate or give up? On a rational level, you know what you must do, but you have developed a routine, a level of comfort, perhaps even an addiction. You've allowed the habit to rule.

Now think about a new activity, one that you would like to begin and know would be good for you such as exercising, dieting, or returning to school. Why is it so hard to get started and stick with it even when you know that to embrace the good and eliminate the bad would bring about a dramatic, healthful change in your life?

Those who succeed understand that success is not just about winning. It is about fulfillment. Success is where joy meets purpose. Social philosopher Charles Handy reminds us that "a worthwhile life requires you to have a purpose beyond yourself."[5] It is essential.

I call those who succeed Leaders of One. They are willing to dig deep and, in so doing, discover purposeful aims. This awareness gives them the strength to face challenges with resiliency and obstacles with innovative thinking, to design a blueprint for action and to carry it out. An added bonus is that as they create a future of their own design, they reduce the uncertainty that has dogged them.

Leaders of One appreciate that the future is never urgent, but it is always important. Because the future will never be urgent, it is easy to postpone. Shaping the future requires disciplined leadership to commit to the long term and patience to overcome the barriers in the present. Think, for example, of the patience displayed by Nelson Mandela, the first South African president to be elected in a democratic election. Before his presidency, he was arrested and sentenced to life in prison. He served twenty-seven years in prison, but he never gave up his dream, never tired of his passion, and never faltered in his belief of reconciliation and the establishment of a multiracial democracy. Mandela never pursued revenge or status.[6] His purpose-driven actions led to the multicultural integration of South Africa and the 1993 Nobel Peace Prize.[7]

By the time something becomes urgent, it is no longer in the future. It is in the present, right in front of us. Now it is a crisis. Having the discipline to act before a crisis occurs is an important aspect of being a Leader of One.

Unfortunately, we live in a society driven by quick fixes, crisis management, instant gratification, and short-term results. This approach is eroding our ability to develop a future-shaping perspective. The need for instant gratification has led many of us to take unhealthy and unethical shortcuts. It has driven many of us to live and work "with the pedal to the metal but the gears in neutral," burning up precious life fuel without making any progress. Such a pace need not be inevitable. We can take steps to break away from it and reconnect with our aim.

These steps make up the framework of this book. It presents a cycle of transformative initiatives that will guide you in shaping your future and enable you to effectively lead the purposes that you wish to advance. The cycle begins with a mental creation and ends with the physical realization of that creation, moving from thought to tangible result. Each of the phases will not by themselves yield better results. They must be taken together and applied in a holistic fashion. They form a system.

The cycle has four phases: (1) Contemplation, (2) Desire, (3) Design, and (4) Creation.

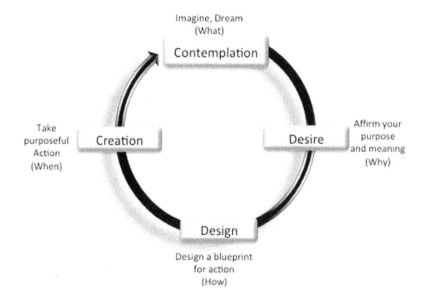

Contemplation. Dedicating ourselves to a period of contemplation forces us to slow down and reflect on our current situation. This process widens and deepens the lens through which we look at the future. If you have ever been on a roller coaster in a theme park, you would agree that it is not the best way to appreciate the landscape below. As you go up and down on the rapid twists, turns, and loops, you experience the exhilaration, but you become oblivious to your surroundings. You are simply hanging on, experiencing the thrill of the ride. But this is not the way to lead your life. It is impossible to shape your future when you are living and working on a roller coaster.

Desire. We need to reassess what we truly want. For it to be sustainable, the future we create must be rooted in purpose and meaning. This stage helps us gauge the strength and intensity of what we want. Here, we articulate the "why" of which we want to pursue.

Design. In this stage, we answer the "how." How are we going to make it happen? We must design a blueprint, just as an architect creates a mockup of a building before starting construction. With a design in place, we can take action.

Creation. Nothing will work without a commitment to action. We can reflect, assess, and design a future for ourselves, but without the act of creation, we have wasted our energies.

Imagine walking into a dark room. You can't see anything, so you turn the lights on. Now you are aware of what is in the room, yet nothing in the room has changed except your own level of awareness. Imagine that the room is a metaphor for your aspirations, your ideal future, and your dreams. You've discovered what they are, but they will become a reality only by taking action.

How should you proceed? This book has been organized to help you follow the process in sequence. A process is defined as a series of activities that transform inputs into outputs. The process espoused in this book does just that. It enables the transformation of imagination, vision, and desires into a tangible design and a design into action. As a result, a new reality is created, a future is shaped. The book is organized around the CDDC cycle, and each chapter contains leadership insights and lessons rooted in my experience working with leaders and teams at the White House, where I worked for over eleven years, the boardroom, and the college campus.

This book advocates that the best learning comes from reflection of experience. In the first section, **Contemplation**, you will be asked to look inward. One task will be to take an inventory of the activities that you've been postponing. You will be asked to begin thinking about your conception of the future. Do you believe that the future is predetermined or something you can control? How you think about the future will impact how you behave in the present.

There is a constant tug of war between who we are and what we do. The chapter "But That's Not Who I Am!" includes an exercise to help you explore the differences.

There are basic themes and key words in this book: dreams, imagination, purpose, leadership, and design. These are critical terms in describing the process of discovery—that which sustains you and justifies who are you, your *raison d'etre*. When Charles Handy was asked where people find their passion, he said, "in dreams"—not just dreams at night but dreams by day. He knew that he had to operate from more than a gut reaction to his dreams. He needed a strategy. Whatever he would dedicate his life to, it had to spring from a sense of mission, an underlying mission. That is what I mean when I speak of purpose.

In the second section, **Desire**, you explore the dynamics of rediscovering what you want. Too often we drift because of the constant pressures of making a living and meeting the demands around us. It's easy to become derailed.

You will be asked to answer questions that may be unfamiliar. For example, what would you do with your time if you did not have to work? Even as a mental exercise, it allows you to consider new themes and possibilities.

When people talk about the "next level," they most often mean moving up in the organization, "climbing the corporate ladder," or getting a promotion, bonus, or tenure. You will read a story about a woman who discovered that achieving the next level was not about moving up but about going deep. Through that exploration, she discovered a purpose that had far more meaning to her and others than simple advancement.

You will examine the question of who is in control of your future. I use the metaphor of the artist and the critic to ask, "Who's painting your canvas?" You will learn from the example that true aims are seldom defined by means but by intents and outcomes. The result of what we do gives meaning to what we do.

If we are open to the world around us, we can find inspiration in the most unusual places. For me, it was Cairo and a taxi driver who forced me to take responsibility for myself. That chapter includes a number of incomplete statements for you to complete. The answers will surprise you.

In the third section, **Design,** you explore your answers to these core questions: "How are your actions and behaviors contributing to creating the future that you want? How do you ensure that your actions are positively influencing others?" Answers to these and similar questions will touch on the connection you have with the rest of the world and the realization that we are all a part of a family that is part of a community that is part of a nation that is part of the world. When the trapped Chilean miners rose one by one to the surface on October 13, 2010, one newscaster noted that the world became one "watching the rescue that had once seemed so distant, so unlikely." Another reporter noted that this wonderful story "transcends national boundaries, transcends national ideology."[8] It was a story that reminded us that we are all in this together.

In another chapter, you will learn about the intrinsic distinction between *reactive, inactive, preactive* and *interactive planning* and their relationships to leading and shaping the future.

How do you plan? Do you go from A to B? What about going from B to A? Are there advantages to creating a mental image of your ideal future and working backward to the present to determine its feasibility? Consciously or unconsciously, we all embrace one type of planning style or another. You will learn about three basic types as well as a fourth that will help you design and create your ideal.

In talking about the power of design, I compare the process to that undertaken when a family designs a house with the help of an architect. It is critical to ask the right questions. How will those around us benefit? How will we ensure that our pursuit is rooted in the common good? Just as architects work to improve a house as a whole, we must stay sensitive to improving our future as a whole. With the use of methods, tools, and exercises, you will learn how to play the role of both family member and architect.

In the final section, **Creation,** I use stories to talk about the challenges of this most difficult stage. I address why we must remain disciplined and committed in the pursuit of an ideal future. For some of us, the process of creation is a test of resiliency, and we may be pushed to give up. Quitting is always an option, but it is the worst one if exercised first. We can't quit when confronted with adversity. What might appear to be a roadblock may actually be a stepping-stone to success.

The future is not a destination or a place. Successful Leaders of One understand that the benefits of pursuing a desired future are more valuable than "arriving." When we think we've arrived, we most likely will begin to decline. We become complacent and bored. The CDDC process is cyclical, designed so that it can begin again in a cycle of perpetual renewal. The love for what you do will enable you to keep performing and advancing.

You cannot shape the future in the future—it must be done in the present. To succeed, you need both leadership and managerial skills. You need leadership skills to "visit" the future, searching for new, fresh connections. You need managerial skills to handle the day-to-day challenges of creating the new present.

In making decisions and taking action, constantly analyze the impact of your behavior. Are you remaining true to your core beliefs? Some basic questions need to be addressed: "What was the difference between my intentions and my results? What role most influenced my actions: my parents, a friend, a colleague, or my boss?"

When we face adversity, when our motives are scrutinized and our knowledge questioned, we must embrace the challenge with trust and the conviction that there is a future worth pursing.

For change to be enduring, we must embrace three domains: the physical, the logical, and the emotional. To neglect one or more is to do so at your peril. Through their integration, hope and wisdom meet. I pose questions to guide you in discovering how the interactions will work to sustain your purpose.

This book is for those who choose to alter the present. It dispels the myth that shaping the future is confined to people with power and authority. It has been my experience that leadership is not merely about rank. The future does not respond to leadership titles but to leadership action. I demonstrate this point using personal and organizational stories that illustrate how people took desire and courage and changed the future in the present.

The book provides the methods; you provide the context.

Transformative change requires courage and the ability to look beyond the seemingly endless demands of today. In so doing, you become your own storyteller. You get to write your own ending and reap the rewards of becoming a Leader of One.

Phase **1**

Contemplation

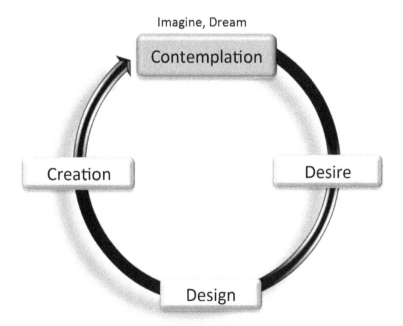

Chapter **1**

The Leader in You

Ultimately, every one of us is a leader, because we all control the attitudes and behaviors of at least one person—ourselves.

—Bob Stevens, Chairman and CEO, Lockheed Martin

In the quote above, Bob Stevens highlights that each person has the power of one. How then can you leverage that power to create a future that reflects your aspirations?

You begin by envisioning what that future can be, but dreams alone will not create a new reality. Nor will luck, knowing the right people, having the right connections, or being in the right place at the right time. Too much is left to chance, to serendipity.

What distinguishes those who have the courage and will to shape their futures from those who are trapped in the present? They develop a Leader of One mindset; they understand that the future cannot be leveraged through sameness, doing the same things in the same old way. They appreciate that the future is not simply an extension of the present.

Technological innovations, medical breakthroughs, and other kinds of advances, as well as setbacks, are changing how the world works and how we interact with it. We communicate in ways unimagined a decade ago. Social networks are not only increasing personal communication, but they are used to accelerate the pace of political revolutions around the world.

What else do these Leaders of One know? They recognize that best efforts and high performance are not enough to shape their futures. Doing work faster or cheaper will not get them there. Greater effectiveness (doing the right thing), not greater efficiency (doing things right), is the critical element.

They accept that success in designing an ideal future requires action and courage. The purpose they wish to pursue, the cause they wish to advance, or the business they wish to expand will require mobilizing others, but first they must mobilize—and transform—themselves.

The real test of a leader is not merely playing a good game today but being able to play in the right game to "win the future." This concept applies to individuals, teams, companies, and even nations.

President Obama introduced this idea in his 2011 State of the Union address.[1] He deviated from the customary address that reflected on a list of accomplishments to emphasize that the country remained strong. Instead, he explained why we must take action now to engage in a discourse, globally and at home, to revitalize our nation's innovative spirit and our entrepreneurial soul. Obama gave the United States a wake-up call and shared the perils of becoming a global bystander. For many, it was uncomfortable to learn how much we've fallen behind in research, education, health care, and infrastructure.

The United States has historically gone beyond what was thought possible. Its leaders in government and business have always understood that dreams require sacrifice, commitment, and perseverance. Our national story is one of translating dreams into action, ideas into patents, products into businesses, and businesses into engines for prosperity. Why then are we falling behind? The question has to be asked if the present course is leading to a future fraught with uncertainty brought on by declining employment, bankrupt institutions, and dwindling resources. Can we hope to offer our children what we have enjoyed in our lifetime?

The pundits pounded Obama's delivery style and his deviation from contemporary presidential addresses to Congress.[2] The style became news, and along the way, an important message was being suppressed: *the fact that success is never about yesterday and how much we've done but about tomorrow and how much we can do.*

A message about shaping the future is compelling. It is hard to argue with the general theme of aspiring to a brighter tomorrow, but how can we? By what method are we planning to shape it? What does it mean to "win the future"? To leverage it? To shape it? At the national level, the "how" becomes hostage to political gridlock. Witness the manufactured crisis over the debt limit in August 2011, and again in September 2013. At the personal level, we meet the future with postponements, excuses, and mental paralysis. In the end, the outcome is the same. We become frustrated with the lack of progress and discouraged about our inability to take the actions that would transform our present.

The future cannot be shaped by talent alone. Shaping is less about skill and much more about courage and the will to lead. It is created when we face and overcome our fears. It is shaped when we discover and articulate a chosen aspiration and pursue it with resolve. It is shaped when we acknowledge the problems ahead. Through that acknowledgment, we can begin to move forward, envision new possibilities, and commit to them.

Or we can do nothing. Doing nothing is a conscious choice. I liken it to someone experiencing high blood pressure who is either unaware of the problem or in denial about it. Without a diagnosis, treatment is postponed, which is why it is often called a silent killer. Reversing it takes an intervention—medication, diet, exercise, or stress management—which will happen only if it is detected in the first place.

The same thing happens to us when we find that we are putting in more effort for less reward or when the cost of living is escalating and we can't keep up. We see our standard of living and quality of life under siege.

The good news is that we can reverse this if we choose to dream and have the courage and will to design and create a future that reflects our desires. The task may seem monumental, but the "how" may surprise you.

Leaders of One engage in transformative initiatives and recognize that they choose their destiny. They recognize that a rewarding future is not a matter of luck but of choice. That realization is liberating, and it frees them to explore possibilities not before imagined.

Maxim: If we keep doing what we've been doing, we will never be able to transcend the present. In an ever-changing world, we cannot leverage the future through sameness. Leaders of One understand that transformation requires courage and action and that the future cannot wait.

Chapter **2**

Taking Charge from Where You Are

To achieve greatness, start where you are, use what you have, do what you can.

—Arthur Ashe, Tennis Player and Philanthropist

Peter Drucker said that "whenever you see a successful business, someone had made a courageous decision."[1] It was courageous because there was probably a great deal of uncertainty supporting the intent, and yet action was taken. A hunch was followed, conventional wisdom defied. Someone was willing to commit to action in spite of the risks. It was done with conviction and with a sense of desire that enabled that person to silence the internal voices of doubt and the external commentary of skeptics.

The former CEO of Southwest Airlines, James Parker, talks about the revolutionary changes that Southwest brought to the airline industry.

Southwest was initially the underdog of the industry and the subject of sabotage by larger competitors. It took desperate measures to stay aloft: a ten-minute turnaround at the gate and offering electronic tickets to eliminate unnecessary expense.

Management placed the highest value on its customers and its employees. Immediately after the terrorist attacks of September 11, Southwest made three key decisions in keeping with its philosophy: there would be no layoffs, no pay cuts, and no-hassle refunds for any customer wanting them. As the rest of the industry bordered on collapse, Southwest remained solvent. Its "market cap soon exceeded all its major competitors combined."[2]

Southwest leaders, and others like them, share certain experiences. They have a vision of what the future can be and the courage to make it happen. They exhibit toughness of character to commit to their aim and the determination to overcome obstructions. These people understand the importance of persuading their stakeholders—venture capitalists, government authorities, educators, business leaders, and even family members—to support them. They take charge of their future by daring to try.

In its most general sense, to lead is to go first. Those who go first must initially imagine a better condition. They go first in creating a pathway to that vision. Their vision is their blueprint. They are first in sharing their beliefs and exemplifying ethical behavior for others. Most importantly, they go first in taking action while putting purpose and outcome ahead of self. Through this fragile process of being first in thought and deed, leaders pave the way to a better future.

Leading is not easy, because any aim worth committing to, any aspiration worth sacrificing for, or any vision worth pursuing brings with it opposition, resistance, failure, doubt, and fear. Decisions about the future are seldom about "this" versus "that," because the options about the future are never explicit. Think of a time when you had to make a tough decision. What was the issue? Try to reconstruct what you considered before taking action. What action did you take? How long did it take you to make a final decision? What made it so difficult? People often say that a tough situation is tough because it was clouded with uncertainty and the risks had an impact on others. That is the reality of creating a better future. It is hard, and often lonely, work.

How do leaders overcome uncertainties to act? They begin with a dream. Everything of importance, like the civil rights movement or landing on the moon begins with a dream. With courage, they imagine what is possible, admit to the impediments that might exist, and formulate actions to challenge them.

Much has been written about leadership within the context of organizations and nations. We tend to confine our notion of leadership to companies, political parties, military units, government agencies, teams, movements, or causes.

In these contexts, those having a high rank are considered leaders. They are expected to show the way and mobilize people to move in a direction to advance a common goal. They are "in charge," having influence over others and accountability for the results. But leadership need not be defined by positions, titles, traits, or skills. Desire and intent are more important. It is not about power but about personal empowerment.

For some people, not having a high profile becomes an impediment to action. They say, "If I were in charge, I would do it differently!" When we don't hold a position of power, it is easy to blame those in charge. Think about your position. What would you do if you were in charge? If you are already in a leadership position, elevate your role above your current rank, and visualize yourself as a CEO, president, principal, dean, chief, or commander. What would you change? What new course would you take? What would you create?

Southwest's James Parker sees leaders everywhere—in large businesses and small, in public and private institutions, in management and labor. "We are all leaders in some way. The example of our behavior is seen and followed by others. We are all communicators of missions and values." [3] If we have the will.

Where is the leader in you? Are you watching the game or playing in it? Are you waiting for others to act, or are you taking charge to influence what happens to you?

Consider how you might answer the following questions:
What compelling aims do you want to pursue?
What in your world would you like to change and why?
Are there impediments? Are they real or imagined?
Where do you place blame when things go wrong?

I casually greet colleagues in the hallway with the customary, "How are you doing?" "Just hanging in there," one says. "Weathering the storm," comments the other. Get the idea? There is a feeling among too many of us that we are little more than human piñatas, taking a beating from life itself. All we can do is to hang on.

Leaders do not wait for things to change before they act. They act now, because they want things to change now. Waiting to be in a position of leadership before taking action can only fuel paralysis. Too often, we postpone the responsibility to act because we are waiting for a promotion, a degree, more experience, or a job change. How many of us believe that "the future will open up once the boss retires"?

Two hundred years ago, the English poet William Wordsworth expressed this sentiment in verse: "The world is too much with us late and soon, getting and spending, we lay waste our powers."[4] At all levels, most of us find ourselves under siege. Many corporate executives today are taking a beating from shareholders, customers, and the economy in general. It is harder to deliver tangible results, to energize others to follow, and the competition is unrelenting. Students are taking a beating as well. They worry about their prospects for success in this tough job market. They are deep in debt and realize the yawning gap between their academic major and their real interests. Like them, we may find ourselves investing time and energy without experiencing genuine success. We are like the piñata, swinging from side to side but no closer to reaching a desired destination.

We can choose to keep doing what we've always done and hope that something better will happen through luck or hard work, or we can choose to dream, design, and create a better future. The stakes are high, but little else matters quite as much.

Maxim: Leaders do not wait for things to change before they take action. They take action now, because they want things to change now.

Chapter 3

Thinking about the Future and Acting on the Present

Let him who would enjoy a good future waste none of his present.

—Roger Babson, American Business Forecaster

Investing your time wisely is critical to shaping your future. The notion of time allocation in future shaping is often neglected, because the present typically takes precedence.

Think of the activities that you perform on a regular basis. Reflect on your daily routine from the moment that you wake up to the moment that you go to bed at night. Now, envision three buckets placed before you. One represents the past, one the present, and one the future. How much of what you do throughout your day belongs in the bucket representing the past? Fixing problems, for example, is all about the past, something that happened yesterday. How much of what you did can be placed in the bucket representing the present? Managing crises would go there. Finally, how much of what you did today, activities such as reflecting and visioning, could be placed in the third bucket?

Regrettably, we spend our days filling up the "past" and "present" buckets. We take time away from the future to deal with the present. By staying rooted in the present, we ensure that things will never change.

It sounds paradoxical, but a "good" present begins in the future. It begins with your statement of desire, the articulation of your vision. If you do not like where you are at this moment, it's because at some point in the past you neglected the future. You did not do anything to prepare for a better future, and thus you arrived at a point where you do not want to be.

The opposite is also true. A good future begins in the present, because in the present, we can take action. Futurist Joel Barker reminds us, "If we neglect the future, we will never have a good present. But if we neglect the present, we will quickly run out of our future." [1] We cannot shape the future in the future. We must take action today and we must know what kind of action to take.

It is a common error to tweak the present, make marginal improvements, and think that the job is done. This is safe and easy, but it is also unproductive. We may stagnate or decline. We may become comfortably numb, like teachers who do not embrace the latest instructional methodologies or research because they are too comfortable with the methods from the past. We behave like the company that continues to extend the lifecycle of an old product line without creating anything fresh. The company loses its market share because it didn't invest in the future and didn't innovate or act on its own innovation. Kodak exemplifies this. It invented the digital camera in 1975, but its success with film photography prevented it from exploiting its own creation and leading the way to a new paradigm of photography. Unfortunately, Kodak filed for bankruptcy on January 19, 2012. [2]

Innovation is critical as we design our future. Design efforts require us to reflect and to contemplate as we scout the environment for new connections, ideas, and possibilities. Innovation requires leadership on our part, the ability to "pull" the future into the present and "push" the present out to meet it.

While leadership actions are *systemic* and holistic, managerial ones are *systematic* and disciplined. Both are needed for progress, but we need leadership skills first so that we can mentally create and then "visit" the future. In contemplation of the future, we find inspiration, hope, ideas, and opportunities to help us create a new present.

We also need management skills. They help us develop timelines, deal with logistics, allocate resources, and monitor progress. We need these skills to complete a goal on time and within budget. These activities are important, but their value is contingent on our strategic intent. What is our goal? Why, and why now? Management activities are useless in the absence of answers to these questions. A Chinese proverb reminds us that "tactics without vision are noise before defeat." If we remain in the present, we will lose touch with our primary role, which is to create the future and pull it into the present.

In an organizational context, rank and title offer a clear demarcation of leadership and managerial roles. Once organizational leaders design a blueprint for the future, they hand it off to those responsible for implementing it and "pushing the present out." When it relates to ourselves, we must shift from leading our future to managing our present without letting either perspective dominate or suppress the other. There is no handing off responsibility to others.

The shift we must make between leading and managing our future represents a push-pull dynamic. Pulling the future into the present calls for some degree of boldness, attending events that are outside of our usual experience and studying material outside of our field. In so doing, we prepare ourselves in the present to become comfortable with what is new and unfamiliar, and we are less apt to let uncertainty undermine our determination.

We must make time for reflection during these push-pull activities. We need to ask ourselves the kind of questions that place us in the future such as "Wouldn't it be nice if…? What if I tried…? What is keeping me from doing…?" The primary job of a leader is to shape the future. Seeking the answers will serve as a catalyst for shaping your future.

How often do you find yourself thinking about the future or questioning whether things will get better over time? Have you ever felt impatient to know what the future will bring? Are you obsessed with thinking about the future?

When I ask executives in class how many believe that the future is important, almost all raise their hands. When I ask how many of them are constantly thinking about tomorrow, I get the same results. Then I ask them where they learned how to create the future: in school, at home, at work, or at the university? There is typically no reply to this question, and they seem dumbfounded by it. When I ask how many have taken a course on designing and shaping the future, almost no one raises a hand.

Most of us spend a great deal of time thinking about where we will be in five, ten, or twenty-five years, yet the future is something we rarely address in a formal way. Why is it that the very thing we think about so often, the thing we claim is important to us, is something for which classes or guidelines are rarely if ever offered?

In a survey conducted with executives from Lockheed Martin Corporation, the notion of shaping the future emerged as one of the most important responsibilities and one of toughest things that a senior leader does in an organization, and yet it is considered one of the most neglected tasks.[3] The same is true for individuals. We recognize the imperative of shaping our own future, but we often neglect it.

As you will learn in this book, the future is never urgent, and thus it is easy to postpone. We clutter our day with irrelevant tasks and activities but seldom carve out the time to work on what will help us build a better future. The tyranny of mundane routines suppresses our capacity to engage in future-shaping activities.

The uncertainty associated with the future can be paralyzing. When we hear the statement, "You never know what the future holds," it is easy to envision adverse situations or project negative outcomes. In trying to avoid the negative, we may become so concerned with how the decisions we make today could lead to irreversible consequences that we suppress our desires and drift into hyperanalysis, inaction, fear, and anxiety. Ultimately, we fail to take action in the present and end up further from the future we want.

If thinking about a negative future can lead to paralysis, I suggest that the opposite can also be true. If we focus on a compelling vision and anticipate its positive outcomes, we will be inspired, empowered, and mobilized to take action.

A positive and fervently desired image of the future is essential to translating patterns of fear into patterns of trust and patterns of doubt into patterns of hope. As the Austrian psychiatrist and Holocaust survivor

Viktor Frankl noted, "Thinking about the future in positive terms is energizing, motivating, and a critical differentiating factor among nations, companies and individuals who excel and succeed." [4]

The mindset we have toward the future, and the methods we use to approach it, are crucial in taking ownership of our destiny and in mitigating the anxieties associated with uncertainty. We must believe that what happens between now and the future depends mostly on what we do, not on what is done to us.

We respond, perhaps unconsciously, to the notion that the future is inevitable, but it is empowering when we conceive of it as a blank slate. The first challenge is to make shaping our future a priority, and the second challenge is to change our conception of the future. If we approach it with the mindset that the future is subject to creation, we can shape it.

Pause now and make a list of all activities, routines, or tasks that you've been postponing even though you know they would help you progress toward a desired goal. Now make a list of the obstructions that make it difficult to undertake those activities. What is the source of these obstructions? Are they real? Do they include the lack of a degree or a declining job market for your skills? Are they more psychological? Is fear underlying your ability to take action? When you think about why you are not taking steps toward building your future, are your statements excuses in disguise?

Now take a moment to think about your conception of the future and how it might affect your conception of the present.

- Do you see the future as predetermined and inevitable, or do you believe that the future can be created?

- Do you think that things in general were better in the past? Do you look to the past for inspiration and solutions?

- Are you frequently forecasting the future based on the past?

- Do you give serious thought to tomorrow, or are you satisfied with the status quo?

Throughout this book, we will revisit these and other questions and their implications. For now, reflect on them and start formulating answers. Sociologist John Schaar noted that the future is not some place to which we are going but one that we are creating. The paths to it are not found but made, and the activity of making them *changes both the maker and the destination.* [5] The power is in us.

Maxim: Your concept of the future is a matter of choice. The way you think about the future will impact how you act in the present. The primary job of a leader is to shape the future, not to fix the past or manage the present. We can't shape the future in the future. We must pull the future from our imagination and take action in the present to make it a reality.

Chapter 4

When Slow Is Fast and Down Is Up

There is more to life than increasing its speed.

—Mohandas Gandhi, Indian Nationalist Leader

It seems as if the time between the present and the future has shrunk. The future used to take longer! Technological changes that used to define a generation now happen within months. The remarkable speed at which new knowledge can be created and disseminated is reshaping our world.

It is stunning to embrace the fact that the Google search engine gets over 2.5 billion hits a day.[1] Consider also the fact that all of the world's trade in 1949, all of the foreign exchange dealings in 1979, and all of the telephone calls made around the world in 1984, now happen in a single day. It feels like "a year in a day."[2]

Forty years ago, Alvin Toffler published a book that anticipated how this acceleration of change would redefine us. He describes a psychological disease that he called "future shock." In the book by the same name, he said, "Much that now strikes us as incomprehensible would be far less so if we took a fresh look at the racing rate of changes that makes reality seem, sometimes, like a kaleidoscope run wild. For the acceleration of change does not merely buffet industries or nations. It is a concrete force that reaches deep into our personal lives, compels us to act out new roles, and confronts us with the danger of a new and powerfully upsetting psychological disease. This new disease can be called 'future shock.'" [3]

In spite of all the technological breakthroughs and an increase in the standard of living in most industrialized nations, we seem to have an unquenchable thirst for more. People are literally lining up for hours to acquire the latest version of a game or cellphone. We want faster, cheaper, virtual, three-dimensional, holographic, surround, and nano. Cellphones have become carry-in-your-pocket computers. We are developing TV remotes that rely on voice recognition rather than buttons. A researcher who is leading the effort for this device said, "It's something that even one-year-olds can understand." [4]

Technology allows us to stay linked with friends, family, and the world in ways we could not have imagined twenty years ago. We are becoming a global community of technophiles, eager to adopt a new language that lets us communicate faster with fewer keystrokes.

Google seemingly tries to read our minds. If we type "global" into its search bar, we are given a list of options: *global agenda, global warming, globalization, global visionaries,* and so on. If Google guesses right, we are a click away from our destination. Google is now a verb, as in "I'll Google that and get back to you." Scientists at Google are developing technologies to develop autonomous cars that they believe will transform transportation as profoundly as the Internet transformed communications. They believe that "robot drivers react faster than humans, have 360-degree perception, and do not get distracted, sleepy, or intoxicated." [5] Think about it.

Do you have any secrets left? Amazon knows what you like to read and buy. When you order a book, Amazon reminds you of book titles that have similar themes or other books by the same author. When you pay at a grocery store, the receipt contains coupons for items you bought in the past.

We spend our days in front of a screen. According to Nielsen, in 2002, the average American spent fifty-two hours a month on home computers; today that number is sixty-eight hours a month.[6] A Kaiser Family Foundation study found that kids are spending an average of more than seven and a half hours a day, seven days a week, using all forms of media. That translates to more than fifty-three hours a week—more time than their parents spend at work. The same study found a link between media use and poor grades: 47 percent of heavy users (those using media more than sixteen hours a day) reported getting grades of C or lower.[7]

With children growing up with push-button technology, they don't learn basic skills at an appropriate age: how to zip up a jacket, how to tie their shoes before entering first grade, or how to operate a can opener or get ice cubes out of a tray by the time they're teenagers. They do not learn how to write in cursive.[8] Mark Bauerlein, author of *The Dumbest Generation*, argues that kids growing up today don't develop the skills needed to figure things out for themselves, which leads to a "loss of independence and a loss of initiative."[9]

This pace of change affects all of us in unintended ways. We multitask because our digital world allows us to. We see it at the gym. People wear headphones as they jog, listen to music or a book on tape, and take business calls while watching the stock market prices stream by on TV.

Are we really getting more done? What is the downside to multitasking? Scientists have learned that as we multitask, we do each task more poorly than if we had tackled each one by itself, and those who multitask the most do the worst. The National Academy of Sciences reported on a Stanford University study comparing heavy and light multitaskers. Heavy multitaskers have difficulty ignoring irrelevant information, and they can't switch as quickly from one task to another.[10] Although heavy multitaskers love information, their thrill is in getting more and more of it. Low multitaskers, on the other hand, would rather spend their time thinking about the information they already have. They value reflection.

Scientists at the University of California-San Francisco found that only when rats take a break from their explorations are they better able to process their experiences and create a memory of them. The scientists contend that when a brain is constantly stimulated, the learning process is forfeited.[11] *Down time is, indeed, up time.*

These devices can also be lethal, which is why states are enacting new laws forbidding the use of handheld devices and texting while driving. People are run down by speeding vehicles as they read their e-mail in the middle of a crosswalk, unable to hear the traffic because of their iPods. In September 2008, we read of a Los Angeles Metrolink train engineer who failed to stop at a red signal because he was exchanging text messages, and twenty-five people died in the crash.[12]

We are sacrificing any sense of decorum and of keeping what's private private for the sake of staying connected. We carry on conversations while ordering a meal, waiting in line for the grocery scanner, and at the doctor's office. Some commuter trains have "quiet cars" to protect riders who prefer to read and work in silence. We overhear phone conversations that make us blush, and if we ask someone to "keep it down" or take the phone outside, we are chastised.

It's fair to ask this question: Are we better off because of these technological breakthroughs? In a big sense, we are, when we think of all the advances in science, engineering, and medicine. We recognize that technology allows us to access information faster and more accurately and to be able to work virtually anywhere. We are no longer chained to our desks. Electronic communication today is almost instantaneous, saving valuable time that we can devote to more productive pursuits.

Are these platforms making our lives better, more creative, more productive, or more healthful? Are they ensuring for us a better future, or are they simply offering technological amusement? Where does technology belong in our lives as we think about who we are, where we are, and where we want to go? Technology unquestionably makes it possible for us to move faster and do more, but it is essential not to confuse technical connectivity with human connectedness.

Saint James, the Catholic patron of Spain, asked of himself and others, "What good is speed if the brain has oozed out on the way?"[13] Media powerhouse Oprah Winfrey revealed in a 2013 interview with *Access Hollywood* that during the time she was filming *The Butler*, she nearly had a meltdown. "In the beginning, it was just sort of speeding and a kind of numbness and going from one thing to the next thing to the next thing." She added, "I remember closing my eyes in between each page because looking at the page and the words at the same time was too much stimulation for my brain."[14] She felt overwhelmed by the fast pace, the intensity, and the reach of her daily agenda.

Take a minute to reflect on the pace of your life. Has your brain "oozed out" on the way? Are you making great time but don't know where you're going?

The following exercise will help you determine how fast you are traveling. I use the metaphor of a train trip, because it's something we've all experienced and it has a destination. Find a quiet place, read the passage below, and then close your eyes and reflect on the trip as you see it.

You are on a speeding train. You see the blur of tree branches outside as they whiz past and a line of graffiti that blends into one. As the train continues, you pass neighborhoods and towns, each a dot that appears and disappears as you barrel ahead.

Now picture this train as a metaphor for your life. Look out the window and think about what you saw. Did you appreciate the views? Did you feel as though you were gaining ground on the week's bombardment of meetings, deadlines, e-mail, voice mail, instant texts, phone calls, and family engagements? Was it a feeling of satisfaction and fulfillment, of validation for your hard work, or did you feel overwhelmed, knowing that next week will be the same? Now look around you. Do you recognize those riding with you? Are you in good company?

It is not uncommon for people to get caught up in life's daily events and demands and become oblivious to all else. We may get so caught up by the pace that we lose sight of why we are even headed in a particular direction. Do we know what we're going to do when we get there? Is it really important to get there on time? Did we set the time of arrival, or did someone else? We can become so distracted along the way that we fail to appreciate the panoramic views or the people riding with us.

Many people are riding fast on the wrong train. They are "making good time" in terms of earnings, promotions, and status, but they are no longer thinking about the basic questions that would reassure them of the rightness of their direction. As the speed of the train—their life—gains momentum, they surrender to the flow.

Technology plays a role in driving us to ramp up our productivity. It is estimated that people today consume three times as much information each day as they did in 1960.[15] That number is astonishing. How can we retain that much data and make sense of it?

Research shows that computer users at work change screen windows, check e-mail, and shift to other programs nearly thirty-seven times an hour. Scientists are finding that being routinely exposed to such bombardment and hyperstimulation changes how we think and behave. More alarming is the finding that our fractured thinking and lack of focus on a single activity persists even after we have logged off, which has a damaging effect on our work and our lives.

We are never in the moment. It is hard to slow down and reflect on what is going on. Demands for our time and our energy don't diminish, and regrettably, the awareness may come to us not by choice but by necessity. We have an accident, get sick, lose a job, or a loved one dies. How much better would it have been to apply the brakes and recheck our direction, to put our internal GPS to work to recalculate the route, speed, and time of arrival?

Slowing down requires recognizing that it is important to do so. Instead of sitting passively as a passenger on a speeding train, we need to move to the front of the train and become the engineer. As we slow the train down, what do we see? The images out the window are no longer blurs but detailed vistas, landscapes of our own creation.

It is not morbid to ask ourselves how we want to be remembered and what we would like our legacy to be. If the "train" we are on is not going to get us there, we may decide to hop off at the next station. We can begin the act of contemplation, of reflection and recreating the dreams we've been postponing. The narrative lies within all of us, but it will emerge only as a result of contemplation and reflection. This process is impossible if we do not slow down.

I am not suggesting abandonment of our duties and responsibilities. I am suggesting creating a mental space, creating the equivalent of a train stop that will bring a renewed perspective. Then you can reboard, knowing that this will be the ride you enjoy the most. This is, after all, the ride of your life.

Maxim: Be aware that speed and progress are conceptually distinct but are experientially intertwined. When absorbed by the rapid pace of contemporary life, we could easily confuse means with ends. Though valuable and advantageous, technology is no substitute for the strength of the human spirit. Purpose, intent, and desire are by far more powerful than computing power. Slowing down and discovering your desired direction will give you the ultimate foundation for progress and fulfillment.

Chapter **5**

The Past Is Not What It Used to Be

Those who cannot remember the past are condemned to repeat it.

—George Santayana, Spanish Philosopher, Essayist, Poet and Novelist

Most people recognize the quote above. It first appeared in 1905 in the essay "The Life of Reason: or The Phases of Human Progress," published by the Spanish-born American philosopher George Santayana.[1] When you read it, do you think about the past or the future?

Many believe that Santayana was focusing on the past, but he was offering insight into the future. Imbedded in this thought is an implicit question: If we are not condemned to repeat the past, then what? If we are not condemned to repeat the past, then the future is subject to creation. We have an opportunity to shape it.

The failures of the past contain many important lessons. Santayana conveys that if we wish for a brighter future, we must learn from the mistakes that we, or others, have committed.

A popular definition of insanity is repeating the same action but expecting a different result. As Santayana warns, ignoring the past can doom us to repeat mistakes, because we are carrying out the same unsound practices. Be that as it may, failure can become a springboard for discovery.

When we fail, we confront the challenge of finding a better way. We should not ignore mistakes—they contain powerful lessons that will help us create something new.

It is important to note that while we must learn from the past, we cannot anchor ourselves to it. We cannot allow what took place to prevent us from creating a different present and future. Presidential biographer David Maraniss asked President Bill Clinton, "Mr. President, do you believe in life after death?"[2] In a reflective manner, the president paused and said, "I have to. I need another chance."

This response is not necessarily one that conveys the power and strength of the commander in chief, but it conveys the struggles, vulnerabilities, and humility of a human being seeking a second chance. President Clinton understood that his actions would be part of his history, and there was little he could do to change that fact. Still, it seemed that he understood he was not doomed to fail in the days ahead. A "second chance" represented the opportunity to create a future that would give redeeming value to his presidency and his life. Like President Clinton, it is up to us to give meaning to the past and use it to build a future. We can never let the past take precedence over the present.

What if the past was a good one? Wouldn't we want to remember it, extend it, and replicate it? What is wrong with repeating what was a good thing? Lew Platt, former CEO of Hewlett-Packard, cautioned, "Whatever made you successful in the past won't in the future."[3] Sobering words. In fact, past success oftentimes serves as the pathway to failure, because we become complacent. The conditions that led to past success are often impossible to replicate because of the multiplicity of factors involved at the time. Success cannot be replicated free of context. It is like trying to replicate the success of a real estate transaction. You can replicate to exacting standards all the steps of the process, yet the results will vary greatly because you are executing the transaction in a new economic context.

Good memories can have enormous influence over us. They hold great intrinsic value, but it is important that they do not get in the way of what is still in wait for us. Our accomplishments should never outshine our potential for a better future.

We must welcome the future, noted Santayana, "remembering that soon it will be the past; and we must respect the past, knowing that once it was all that was humanly possible."

Our actions in the present will give shape and direction to our future. Thus, *if* we are not condemned to repeat the past, the future is our second chance to create a better way. Possibilities will emerge and opportunities will be revealed. As Thomas Paine wrote in *Common Sense,* "We have it in our power to begin the world over again."[4]

Maxim: Remember just enough of the past to capture its wisdom and avoid the same pitfalls. Forget just enough of it so that you can unleash yourself from it and create what the future can be.

Chapter 6

But That's Not Who I Am!

The first and best victory is to conquer self.

—Plato, Classical Greek Philosopher

My undergraduate student, Elliott, was an attentive and introspective learner, wise beyond his years and a true contributor to the learning experience. At the end of one class, he approached me and said, "Dr. Suárez, there is a simple exercise I think will contribute to uncluttering our thinking and help us connect with our core." I was curious and, after listening to the description, asked him if he would be willing to facilitate this exercise at our next session.

At the beginning of the next session, I introduced Elliott, and he took it from there. He delivered the exercise to the class in the following way. (Feel free to try it with a partner.)

"This is an activity to discover something about ourselves, about our own identity. I would like all you to select a partner, and for several minutes Partner A will stare into Partner B's eyes and repeat the sentence 'I blank,' followed by the

phrase, 'but that is not who I am.' In the blank space, say different things that are true about yourself. For example, 'I am an engineering student, but that is not who I am.' Fill in the blank with things that you think are true about yourself, even with activities you engage in and the perceptions others have of you. Partners A and B must 'lock eyes' and not look away as the other is sharing the information. Doing this raises the challenge of the activity. Try not to look away. After two minutes, switch to Partner B, go for two minutes, and then switch again, going back and forth."

The students quickly paired up, and the class sounded a bit loud, chaotic. It was hard to discern the various conversations. I started to roam around the room and heard things such as, "I was born in Maryland, but that's not who I am." "I am an honors student, but that's not who I am." "My father is a lawyer, but that's not who I am." "I have three siblings, but that's not who I am." They continued, but at the three-minute mark, something interesting began to happen. The students were taking more time to think about their next descriptor. Their voices lowered, and after seven minutes, there was almost complete silence.

Elliott had not asked them to stop, but the reflection process led them to think deeper and deeper about who they really were. As they chipped away at the superficial attributes, they were confronted with the notion that "if I am not all of those things, then who am I?"

The conversation took a new twist. They were beginning to think from the inside out, not the other way around. "I'm optimistic." "I am giving." "I am dedicated." "I am fearful." "I am curious." Little by little, they were connecting with something deeper and abandoning the end of the sentence ("but that's not who I am"). What was left was a description, or at least the beginning of one, of their core, stripped of external labels.

For most people, the exercise is awkward. Making constant eye contact while talking about yourself is not as easy as it sounds. For most, it is easiest to deny titles, work, the organization they work for, hobbies, and even personal traits, but when asked what was hardest to deny, most agreed that it concerned faith, family, beliefs, and values. These represent the basis of how we see the world. These are the elements we hang onto in tough times and think most about when experiencing challenges. They are essential for moving from aspiration to action. They are the core traits that help us transform ideas into design and design into creation.

Bob Stevens, former CEO of Lockheed Martin, understands the implications of having a strong core, even for a multinational organization. He suggests, "Change is only brought about by people, and people are not inspired, engaged or motivated by process or procedure. People move to values, vision, principles, basic beliefs about who we are."[1]

To begin any transformation, we need to know who we are. We need to identify what we see as our purpose. To do so, we need to make time for ourselves, to ask and answer the tough questions. For success, we need to engage in humble self-reflection, listening carefully to our inner voice and reexamining our motives. We must push ourselves out of our comfort zones. Discomfort is a sign of progress.

Maxim: Who we are is not about titles and possessions but about purpose and consequence. Never let external validation and the perceptions of others dictate who you are. Build your future upon your core principles. They will provide the strength you need to lead and pursue meaningful aims.

Compilation of Contemplation Phase Questions

- Do you think things were better as they were before?

- Do you look to the past for inspiration and solutions?

- Do you give serious thought to tomorrow, or are you satisfied with the status quo?

- How do you handle change, new problems, and challenges?

- Are you frequently forecasting the future based on the past?

- Do you see the future as predetermined and inevitable?

- Do you believe that the future can be created?

- Picture a train as a metaphor for your life. Look out the window and think about what you see. Do you appreciate the view?

- Do you feel as though you are gaining ground on the week's bombardment of meetings, deadlines, e-mail, voice mail, instant texts, phone calls, and family engagements?

- Do you feel satisfaction and fulfillment, validation for all your hard work, or do you feel overwhelmed, knowing that next week will be the same?

- Are you making time to listen carefully to your inner voice?

- When was the last time that you reexamined your motives?

- Are you pushing yourself out of habitual thinking and comfort zones?

Phase 2

Desire

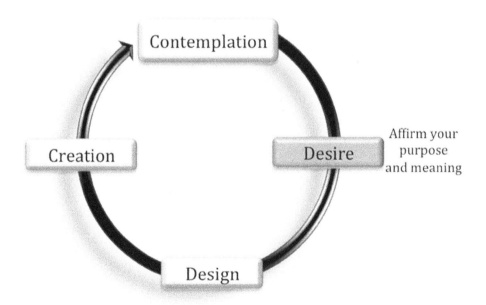

Chapter 7

Find Your Purpose, Nurture Your Passion

Follow your heart, but be quiet for a while first. Ask questions, then feel the answer. Learn to trust your heart.

—Unknown

We are entering the Desire phase of the CDDC cycle. Each chapter in this section revolves around a story to help you reflect and reconnect with a deceptively simple concept: identifying what you want to create or do. This phase is rooted in purpose and passion, something that we all have but few make the time to discover.

Passion is defined as an intense desire or enthusiasm for something—the struggle is finding that "something." People who live their passion attract opportunity and exude energy. They strive to achieve excellence with their unique talents. Their jobs are platforms by which to make contributions to what they believe in and what they enjoy doing.

Passion and purpose are two sides of the same coin. We can view them separately but cannot separate them. As my colleague Vincent P. Barabba suggests, it is not about one *or* the other; it's about one *and* the other.[1] Purpose and passion form a system of meaning and connectedness that allows us to live a fulfilling life, one of impact and consequence.

It is hard to think of a leader who has no purpose or sense of direction. It is impossible to lead without it. Some, however, lack passion, that energy to inspire and mobilize others. Effective leadership requires both.

The winners of the MacArthur Foundation Genius Grant represent that magical pairing of purpose and passion. One winner, Francisco Nunez, has been the artistic director of the Young People's Chorus (YPC) of New York City for decades. "His vision of young voices from inner city to elite schools singing new music of the highest quality underpins all that he does."[2] YPC tours throughout the United States and internationally. Nunez believes that youth choirs can transform lives while expanding artistic boundaries.

Like Nunez, finding your purpose and your passion, your "gift," follows a process of reflection and discovery. It takes time and focus to discover a connection to something deep within. You have to sense it and feel it. There are no wrong answers, only right ones, if they come from you.

Passion is often confused with novelty. When I first started to play golf, I got the "golf fever." I tried to play and practice as much as I could. I read books, watched films, and even found myself practicing the swing without a club in hand. Had I found my passion? Hardly. Golf was too time consuming, and I ended up abandoning it within months. This was not a passion but a fleeting interest.

True passions are enduring. They are driven by something internal. Our passions can evolve and deepen, and they can be renewed. Passions provide continuity to whatever propels us forward.

How do you know if you are living your passion? The questions below seem simple and direct, yet the answers will be profound if you commit to going deep and answering them with sincerity.

- What are you inspired by? Why?

- Who inspires you the most?

- What kind of people do you like to be surrounded by? Why?

- What makes you feel productive?

- What makes you feel that time is flying by?

- When was the last time you experienced happiness? What were you doing?

- What makes you feel proud of yourself?

- What makes you feel proud of your team or your company?

- What would you do if not limited by the need for money?

- What commitment or initiative have you been postponing? How does procrastination make you feel?

- What intrigues you?

- What would you like to know more about?

- What is the one thing you would like to accomplish before you die?

Answer these questions in writing, and revisit them in a few days. Make adjustments if necessary. Remember that you are in a process of self-discovery, and it may take a few iterations before you feel connected with your passion.

I had the honor to serve at the White House during the Clinton and the George W. Bush administrations as director for presidential quality and later as director of organizational development and customer support. I was immersed in one of the most fascinating job environments in the world. I traveled aboard Air Force One and HMX helicopters, visited Camp David, and roamed the White House from East Wing to West Wing.

I was addicted to the fast pace, the mission, the excitement and pressures, the stress, the long days and short nights, and the life on the road all over the world, supporting the most powerful position on earth. I loved my job, and the importance of it was unquestionable, because there were no unimportant jobs in support of the president. Working at the White House became a way of life. I did it for so many years that it left a profound imprint on me.

The people around me had gone through the most stringent background checks that the government conducts. There is no higher security clearance in the nation than that given to those with presidential duty access. Those around me were handpicked, and they formed a team of extremely talented and well-connected people. The stakes were high and so were the egos as they came to work. You felt important, so you found yourself acting decisively. The world was watching.

In spite of all the novelty and the proximity to power, the White House teaches you how humility empowers leadership and why it is never about you but always about a mission, a purpose that transcends any individual. Even presidents are stewards of a higher purpose. They lead not just a nation that protects democracy, but they also protect the notion that the pursuit of liberty and happiness are inalienable rights of the American people.

This connection with purpose grew even stronger after my days at the White House. I was finally able to reflect on what it meant outside of a political milieu. I had been absorbing important insights and was later able to acknowledge them.

For many, it is hard to transition out of the White House, because the institution offers unparalleled strength and clout. Once out of the environment, it is not uncommon to feel vulnerable. When I moved on, I discovered that strength, importance, and job security do not come from a title or a particular position in an organization. Security comes from discovering your passion and effectively using your skills and competence to make a contribution.

I transitioned from the White House into teaching and public speaking engagements at national and international conferences. Teaching energized me. The participants' desire to better their lives gave renewed meaning to my work. I discovered that I loved to teach because it was a way to find connection, to contribute and to give back to those who are our future. This was similar to the overarching aim of the presidential administrations. We can all transition from a current state to the desired one.

Use the following questions to discover and connect with your purpose. Write down your answers, and revisit them in a few days.

- What activities do you enjoy the most?

- What kind of work would you do for free?

- Do you chronically feel tired at the end of each workday?

- What is your "picture" of happiness?

- What is your "picture" of success?

- What gives you a deep sense of satisfaction? Accomplishment?

- What is your "gift"? How are you using it?

- What work or activity do you find most rewarding?

- What contributions or achievements do you find most desirable?

- What issues or causes are you most moved by?

- Which world problem or challenge would you like to see solved?

- How would you like to serve others if time were abundant?

The right answers are never "out there" in terms of position, status, title, prestige, or wealth. When we think that the answer about our true passion lies in external factors and we go after them, we distance ourselves from the object of our search.

You are probably busy and consumed by the load of work that you do. You may also feel that you've gone too far, and you've invested so much time that there is no point in changing your course. A Chinese proverb tells us, "No matter how long you've been on the wrong road, turn back!" Success is an outcome. When you follow your passion, success follows you. You will know when you have connected with your purpose and your passion because you will be moved by it, and so will those whom you touch.

I was talking one day with a colleague, Nancy, about a team of undergraduate students who had created an organization to support orphans in Ukraine, Shutters 4 Scholars[3] (it is described in the chapter "Learning to Lead and Leading to Learn").

This team of business, engineering, computer, and physical sciences students identified a need about which they were passionate. They followed through on the project with ingenuity and commitment to make a difference in the lives of children they did not even know. They successfully applied many of the tools I talk about in this book to create an innovative business model by partnering with a nonprofit organization to deliver real and intrinsic value to the lives of orphans.

Nancy loved the outcome of the project, saying, "It makes me feel good to see that as a business school we are able to do these great things." She loved the fact that the students followed their hearts and then used their minds to make it all happen. She was enthralled by the notion of these students connecting and following through with a passion at such an early stage in their lives. She paused in her discourse and, with a penetrating gaze, asked, "Do you think everybody has a passion? Do I have a passion?"

She caught me off guard. While everyone surely has a passion for something, for many it is buried deep, but the question demonstrated to me that not everyone knows what it is. Nancy is not alone.

Drifting from our passion is often a slow and gradual process, driven by the demands of our present reality. It is generally a corrosive complacency that results in suppression. We may say, "I will do this for a few years, and then I will…" We make compromises and adjustments in what we think we must do to make a living. The sad truth is that daily life can whittle away at what we know to be our purpose in life until it fades from view.

I'm told frequently by students and corporate leaders in my sessions, "I can't afford to stop what I'm currently doing to pursue my dream." The question ought to be whether you can afford *not* to pursue it. What is the cost to you in the end?

How do you know if you are not following your passion? Take a minute to think about the following scenario: *Your employer guarantees your current pay for life, adjusted for inflation. You are told that you are free to do whatever you please; there are no expectations whatsoever and no adverse repercussions.*

What would you do? Would you report to work as usual? If you decide to work, why would you?

Is it because it is now a habit?

Is it because it is the only thing you know how to do?

Is it because of your relationship with the people you work with?

Is it because the job is fulfilling or the cause or mission important?

Is it because it doesn't even feel like work and you love it?

Is it because you feel guilty if you do not show up?

Is it because you fear being bored?

If you would *not* go back, also ask why. What are the reasons? Is it because the job was not fulfilling in the first place? Is it because you want to spend more time with your family? Do volunteer work? Change careers? Travel?

To most of us, the possibility that we can take away the financial aspect of our current jobs lets us consider what we really want to do. We can pursue a course of action because it feels right. It gives us a sense of joy. It nourishes and energizes us.

Removing these constraints, even if simply through a mental exercise, allows new themes and possibilities to surface. If you listen carefully to these themes and reflect on the possibilities, you can find yourself operating from a wholly new perspective. Your self-awareness becomes elevated. You begin to shed those superficial layers—social expectations, professional labels and titles—that not only defined you but caged you.

Before I left Nancy's office, I felt the need to answer her question. "You do have a passion," I said.

"You think so? Where is it?"

"Only you know where it is, and you need to bring it to the surface."

She paused. "I guess you're right, but how do I do that? Do you know how long I've been doing this work? Isn't it a bit late for me?"

Nancy used this conversation to reexamine her life. She did the numbers and realized that she didn't have to work for a living. She also realized that perhaps she was working for the wrong reasons. Work had become habitual. Day to day, she was on "autopilot."

Since our discussion, Nancy has retired from her position and is enjoying life with her family in their second home on the Eastern Seaboard.

She and her husband purchased a Harley-Davidson, and I have not received one more e-mail from her!

Like Nancy, you have a passion but are probably wondering what it is. The following suggestions will help you in your search.

Keep a "passion journal." You might begin by recording each day the most energizing experiences that happened that day. What interactions did you enjoy the most? What kind of activity made the time fly? Which events were emotionally moving or meaningful to you? After a couple of weeks, begin to identify themes. Look for connections, and reflect on what is emerging.

Associate with passionate and creative people. Assess your circle of friends and colleagues. Which ones exude a contagious energy, have a vision, and are confident, daring to lead and succeed? How do you feel when you are around them?

Identify energy killers. What activities drain your energy? What social dynamics, such as unproductive worry or gossip, distract you? What events do you anticipate with apprehension? With enthusiasm?

Ask others. Ask those who are close to you about their perception of you. Select people who are honest and candid. Set the stage for this request so that they feel comfortable sharing their thoughts with you. Ask them about your level of energy. Do they perceive you as conveying enthusiasm, or do you come across as indifferent? Do you speak with a positive or negative voice? Do you see challenges instead of problems? Are you embracing or dismissive of others? Do you listen?

Be grateful, and acknowledge your blessings. Reflect on your strengths and write them down. Are you good with people? Are you trustworthy? Resilient? Resourceful?

Think about the obstacles you've overcome in life. What drove you to succeed? Where did you find the strength to handle disappointment? What helped you get back on track?

Think of your body, your health. Even if it is frail, it has served your well, and you are still alive. Be thankful. Think of your mental capabilities and your potential. Acknowledge how much you have, and be grateful. Persian scientist and poet Omar Khayyam put it best: "Be happy for this moment, this moment is your life." [4]

Imagine your dream realized. Write down a statement of desire, and make it explicit. The more you externalize this statement, the stronger your connection to it will be. Once you do this, it will be hard to let it go.

Notice how your passion manifests itself. Try to sense it and feel it. Is it through pictures, sensations, or ideas? Try to articulate "that thing" that you would like to pursue and for which you would be willing to sacrifice. Imagine the impact of its attainment. Write all of this down.

The output of this reflection becomes input for the next stage in the CDDC cycle. Connectedness with passion is an essential requirement for transformative leadership. Jon Bon Jovi, the American songwriter and actor, noted, "Nothing is as important as passion. No matter what you want to do with your life, be passionate." [5] Passions cannot be learned but can be discovered. This discovery may start with Nancy's question, "Do I have a passion?"

Maxim: Never let habitual routines suppress your passion and fog your gift. We all have a gift, but only a few are wise enough to make the time to find it. When you find your gift, unwrap it, and share it with the world.

Chapter **8**

How Can I Move to the Next Level?

The next level is not about moving up but about going deep.

—J. Gerald Suárez

Laura was a former graduate student, later a colleague of mine, and the consummate professional—meticulous, dedicated, eager to learn, and always willing to help. We worked together for two years at the National Graduate School of Quality Management where I served as chief academic officer and she became dean of students. She later joined a major consulting firm, focusing on quality systems.

In the winter of 2008, as I was catching up with e-mail during the holiday season, I received one from Laura. She was asking for advice on how to take her career to the "next level."

I wondered what level she was talking about. I knew she was on a solid career path, yet her questions reminded me of the many interactions I'd had with students, clients, and colleagues who, in one way or another, were in constant search for that proverbial "next level." I had never met anyone who aspired to achieve the opposite and go down a notch. The "next level" implies moving up and having more, and everyone seems to want to get there. Do they know what they're looking for or what they will do when they get there?

Laura wanted to become renowned in her field of quality management. She wanted to expand her influence, to reach a wider audience. However, life was not presenting her with the opportunities to do so. She was doing her job as best she could and excelling in her field, but there seemed to be no roadmap for heading "up." She began to feel that her career was stagnating.

It is unfortunate that for most people, the "next level" is defined by shallow metrics of success such as possessions and titles. The "next level" should not be driven by a standard of living but by quality of life. It should not be about how much we have but about how much we know, how much we care, and how much we can do to advance a cause higher than our own status. In my reply to Laura, I tried to convey that notion.

> *Laura,*
>
> *The attainment of a certain "level" of status or recognition is not as relevant as the discovery and advancement of a purpose. I have found that the key to success is rooted in identifying the reason why you want to be successful. Typically, successful individuals better themselves and push themselves to new levels of performance because in doing so, they are able to mobilize others toward a purposeful goal.*
>
> *I suggest that you find a way to reflect and connect with something that you are really passionate about. Make an assessment of what kinds of things you would need to know and what positions of influence you would need to acquire to advance your purpose. The driver and inspiration for the next level will come from that passion.*
>
> *Remember that the acquisition of knowledge is like money. Its mere accumulation does not bring about joy. It is only when you share it, when you use it, when you spend it, and when you contribute to a higher cause that you derive intrinsic rewards. The "next level" is rarely about moving up but about going deep. Once you connect with your passion, you will invent ways to get there.*

> *Success is always an outcome, never a goal in itself. Follow your dreams. Make a difference. The outcome of your success will propel you to the "next level."*
>
> *Perhaps this response was more philosophical than you needed, but anything else would be a career advancement gimmick.*

Sincerely,
Gerald

Upon receiving the message, Laura was taken by the notion of depth versus height. She realized that while she had been involved in many efforts throughout her career with the intention of moving "up," none of them achieved the impact that she wanted. She shared the e-mail with her friends and found that all of them agreed with the central message.

After some introspection, she started doing things differently. She shifted her thinking toward going deep rather than up. She told me, "Instead of considering how I could serve myself with my career, I started to consider how I could serve my profession."

She delved into the technical subject matter to gain a deeper understanding of quality management but with an emphasis on supporting something larger than her career.

Laura experienced another shift in her thinking. There was no longer a self-imposed pressure to keep moving "up." She was, in fact, digging deep into the material, deep into her own knowledge, deep into her passion for the field, and deep into the organizations and the people that she wanted to support. She began to relax and realized that when you know what you're talking about, your work and the impact that you create will do your talking for you. There is no need to seek validation through credentials, titles, or awards.

Laura created a path that became clearer to her as she dug deeper into her passion of advancing knowledge and creating positive results for others. She started volunteering her time to local, state, and national associations and groups, and she became active in the speakers circuit. As she was "giving back," her work began to reach audiences that she could only dream of in the past.

As she shared, "The process of going deep may be long, and it is not easy, but ultimately it leads you to personal satisfaction. Most importantly, it allows you to experience your career in ways you may never have imagined."

Maxim: The next level is not about moving up but about going deep. The higher you aspire to go, the deeper the foundation needs to be.

Chapter **9**

Who's Painting Your Canvas?

If you hear a voice within you say "you cannot paint," then by all means paint, and that voice will be silenced.

—Vincent van Gogh, Post-Impressionist Painter

If you had to choose one, would you consider yourself an artist or a critic? Your answer to this deceptively simple question could give you an interesting insight about your attitude and perhaps your approach toward the opportunities and experiences that shape your life and influence your leadership approach.

There are fundamental differences between critics and artists. The dictionary describes a critic as someone who forms and expresses judgment on the merits or faults of something. Critics ponder and react to what is already there. They initiate their work in response to the creations they observe in the external world. They focus on translating their perceptions into commentary and articulating their reactions to an audience.

The artist, on the other hand, is a creator who brings inspiration and passion into the physical world. Artists initiate their work from a more introspective, intangible world. The artist's inspiration is internal, a process of translating emotion into reality. Artists express and nurture their sense of purpose through their work. The output of their effort enables others to reflect and connect with the emotional world represented by the creation.

Being an artist is not easy. Creating something whole and fresh never is. The process itself requires courage and commitment to self-discovery. Picasso noted, "Every act of creation is first an act of destruction." [1] To achieve uniqueness, one must destroy sameness. To achieve breakthrough, one must break with convention, yet distancing one's self from sameness and convention makes one susceptible to the criticism of others and the disinclination to pursue a new path.

I believe that we all have the ability to perform in ways that will make us the "artists" of our own future. We can spend our time blaming, critiquing, and reacting to whatever is "out there," or we can use our talents to paint our own canvas. Our future is like a painter's canvas, a blank slate, a platform upon which we can express ourselves. We can create beauty—in the form of possibilities, hope, aspirations—or we can spend our time as a critic while allowing others and life itself to paint the canvas for us. Michele Cassou and Stewart Cubley, authors of *Life, Paint, and Passion*, observed, "We live in a time in which most people believe there is not much inside them, only what teachers, parents and others have put there." [2]

Imagine that you have a blank canvas stretched before you. Picture this in your mind as you reflect on the following questions:

- What would you like to become?

- What would you like to achieve?

- What would you like to express?

- How would you like that picture to look?

- What impact would you like to have on others?

- What will truly fulfill your aspirations?

- What would you like your legacy to be?

Alison, one of my students at the University of Maryland, came to my office and asked me if I had a minute. Such requests for "a minute" often precede the sharing of something. I feel a level of intensity and emotion in these requests.

Alison majored in accounting and was an honors student. By the time of our meeting, she had completed all the requirements for graduation. She was an exemplary student, an active leader on campus, and a mentor to other students. She possessed a pleasant, slightly introverted personality and was a particularly insightful and reflective student.

"What can I do for you?" I asked.

She paused and then murmured, "I don't know." After a few seconds, she broke her silence. "I'm about to graduate, and I'm not sure what to do next." With her accounting major and academic achievements, she would have no problem finding employment. A next logical step for her would have been to pursue a job related to her major or to pursue graduate studies.

"Have you looked for a job?" I asked. She admitted to searching a bit but was not eager to start a career in accounting.

"How much do you love accounting?"

"Why would you ask me that?"

"Well, I don't sense excitement here. You should be looking forward to your options. People choose a field for different reasons. Some people choose to study a particular discipline because they are interested and passionate about that field, others because they think they could make lots of money, others because they are trying to please someone important to them, others..."

In a tone that bespoke anger, she interrupted me. "I hate accounting! That is my problem."

"When did you find that out?"

"I knew early on. I went into it because my mother is an accountant. She had this expectation about me, and I was afraid of doing otherwise. After all, my parents were paying for my education. I don't want to work as an accountant, but I can't do this to them, right?"

"Are you willing to do this to yourself? Which is worse? This is your life, your future. I think you know what you need to do. The question is whether you have the courage to do it."

People like Alison, who allow others to paint their canvas, are giving away their hopes and dreams. They're surrendering their aspirations and becoming derailed by the tyranny of what *seems* right, not what *is* right. They enter the world of work seeking validation through external rewards, while in their souls they are dampening the fires of their dreams.

Just like Alison, managers and workers in all fields of endeavor struggle between what they really want to become and what they are currently doing. They live with frustration. They put up with a job that doesn't satisfy, dread new opportunities and conditions they can't stand, and rationalize their circumstances. It becomes easy to assign accountability for their problems to other factors: the economy, the job market, their boss, their colleagues, the team, or even their families. They place blame outside of themselves, but the real answer to their malaise lies within.

An executive director at a Fortune 500 company pulled me aside during the break of a strategy session. He shared the news that he had been targeted to become the vice president of a business unit. I congratulated him enthusiastically, but his mood and reaction were not celebratory. "Tell me more," I said.

"I've seen what it is like at that level," he said. "It is bad for me as it is, and I cannot imagine increasing the intensity." As I listened attentively, he went on. "Expectations are surreal, the margin of error narrower, the pressures to deliver results are immitigable. There is no work-life balance. I want to enjoy my family. I'm content right now."

"Can you turn this opportunity down?" I asked.

"I can't. It would send the wrong signal to the leadership. I'm trapped in my own success."

We met again during lunch, and I asked him to think about his ideal scenario. "It is too late for me," he said. He was too concerned about the blowback from turning down the offer and the reaction of his leadership team.

This was no different from Alison's situation. Alison was fearful of her mother's reaction to the fact that after four years of subsidizing an expensive college education, she would learn that her daughter hated accounting.

Alison said, "This will devastate her, this will kill her." Sobbing, she described her mother's reaction, even though it had not taken place yet.

How could she know how her mother would react? As Alfred Hitchcock said about the psychological effect of his films, "There is no terror in a bang, only in the anticipation of it."[3] Anticipation of a fearful event becomes a distracting force that robs us of our capacity to excel and weakens our decision-making potential.

Alison told me more about what she really wanted to do. She became excited about her options, and as the conversation progressed, I saw a glow in her face. She was beginning to conceptually "paint her canvas," and I was able to see the "color" of joy!

She continued sharing her dreams with me and, in doing so, was empowering herself, taking ownership of her canvas. This was an important first step. She gave me a big bear hug. "Thank, thank, thank you!" She extended her arms as if she wanted to fly. "You helped me more than I could have ever imagined."

Two days later, I received an e-mail from her: "Dear Dr. Suárez, reflecting on our conversation, I realized that I knew all along what I had to do. I had 99 percent of the solution but I was lacking that final 1 percent. Thank you for helping me find the 1 percent that I was lacking. It will not be easy, but I'm not afraid to make the right choice anymore."

Months later, Alison returned to the school to facilitate two workshops that she designed to help students envision their future. She wanted to elevate their sense of awareness about the links between the decisions that they were making and the goals that they had set for the future. It was her way to not only give back to others and to share her experience but to keep herself on target with what she was passionate about—people, not numbers!

Alison shaped her future and is leading others to shape their own. Currently she leads her own business, creating coaching relationships that help people realize their goals and move toward their dreams. As for the executive director, he accepted the VP position. His canvas was painted for him, and his imbalanced life is now a reality.

Maxim: Be the artist of your life's canvas. Pick up the brush, and paint the picture of who you wish to become.

Chapter **10**

Egyptian Wisdom

To live is to choose, but to choose well, you must know who you are and what you stand for, where you want to go and why you want to get there.

—Kofi Annan, Secretary-General of the United Nations

In the spring of 2005, I traveled to Cairo, Egypt, to teach an accelerated MBA program to the dean and a group of faculty members from the Islamic University of Gaza. This politically stressed region benefited from a program inspired by the notion that "education, not bullets" would help people shape their future.[1] The train-the-trainer program for the faculty prepared participants to experience the foundations of an MBA program. We used simulations and systems thinking to integrate various disciplines (e.g., accounting, finance, marketing, operations, and logistics) into a cohesive whole.

A philanthropist passionate about bringing hope through education sponsored this program to help the students of Gaza who, after completing their bachelors' degrees in business, could not find jobs. The accelerated MBA program was designed to increase their opportunities in the marketplace. The philanthropist who funded the students' education did so with the precondition that companies in the region would guarantee them employment once they completed the program.[2]

The sessions were rigorous and intense. They were also designed to enable participants to honor their religious practices at their customary times. I traveled with two colleagues, and I barely had time to do anything but teach, but it would have been unforgivable to visit such an incredible country without taking the time to appreciate its rich culture and history. We altered the teaching schedule so that each of us could take some time off.

The hotel made arrangements for a man named Samir to serve as my driver and tour guide. On the morning that I met him, Samir greeted me enthusiastically. With a strong, deep, robotic-like voice, he said, "It is my great pleasure to meet you, sir. I am Samir, and I will make sure that you have a memorable tour." He told me that he was also a history teacher. Working as tour guide was a source of additional income and a way for him to use his teaching and language skills in a different setting, the tourism industry.

I hopped in the car, and Samir asked me what I would like to do. I had no answer, so I asked him for recommendations.

"Mr. Geraldo, I can take you to the Papyrus Museum where you can learn about and see the entire process of crafting the papyrus." I concurred.

His teaching skills kicked into high gear. Within seconds, he was giving me a lesson on how developing a written language helped ancient Egyptians make the leap from *prehistory* (before writing) to *history*. In the abundant papyrus reed, which grows in fresh water along the Nile, they found a medium other than stone for inscriptions. Samir told me that papyrus may have been used as early as 4000 BC.

He was driving along while telling me about the papyrus, so I believed that he had chosen what we should do. It sounded like an interesting site. The Papyrus Museum was, indeed, the right thing to see.

Samir began to talk about the Nile River. "I can also take you to the River Nile, if you wish. I think that would be very nice, because it is a nice day. You seem tired, Mr. Geraldo, and maybe the river will be relaxing for you. We can have a cup of coffee while we walk, and I can tell you facts about the river, but only if you wish. Did you know that water is important not just because it is good for drinking and irrigation but also because the river has the ability to produce extremely fertile soil? This rich soil made it easy for cities and civilizations to spring up along the river banks."

I had been going with the flow, but I became concerned. Samir was driving in heavy traffic, lanes on the road seemed to have no purpose, and every opening on the road seemed to be fair game to go for it and advance. Drivers used their horns to communicate some obscure, encrypted communication system that only they understood. It hit me that I was by myself with someone I did not know and going to no predetermined destination with no means of communication. My priorities shifted to security.

As he continued to drive, I said, "Samir, why don't we go to the Papyrus Museum?" I wanted us to settle on something.

Samir had other ideas. "But Mr. Geraldo, there are other options. I can also take you to the Khan el Kahlili."

That did not sound good to me. While I could relate to the Nile and the papyrus, I could not relate to this foreign name. "What is that, Samir?"

"It is an ancient market and one of the most unique places to visit. It dates back to 1382. It was established during the time when the Fatimids ruled Egypt. It is famous for its ancient streets. I can help you bargain for clothes, artifacts, and spices for your family in America. Do you have children, Mr. Geraldo? I can help you get good deals, if you wish."

Samir made his final offer. "I can also take you to the pyramids of Giza, if you wish. These are one of the Seven Wonders of the Ancient World. I'll be happy to go with you inside, if you wish. You'll see the mummies and appreciate the architecture of these magnificent structures. When we exit, we can see Great Sphinx of Giza, which is the largest monolith statue in the world."

It all sounded amazing, but choosing which site to visit was made even more difficult, because I had limited time to see them and no clue about the distance or time between them. I explained this to Samir and asked him how to go about picking.

"It is simple," he said. "You need to decide what you want. That is all you need to do." He expanded on his reply. "Once you tell me what you want, I will find the fastest and safest route. That is my job and my responsibility, but it is yours to decide what you want. I cannot tell you where you want to go."

I decided to see the Pyramids of Giza and the Great Sphinx. We had time for both, and what an experience that was. For Samir, it was just one more day at a location he had been to many times. He shared with me all kinds of historical facts about the pyramids. I don't remember the details, but I'll never forget the wisdom of his advice, "Only you can decide what you want."

This advice resonates with me today, and I call it Egyptian Wisdom— the notion that no one can decide what we truly want for ourselves. The underlying principle is that we cannot "outsource" our desires and interests, and if we don't know what we are seeking, it is our responsibility to find out. Now I know why Samir ended every recommendation with the caveat, "if you wish."

This lesson applies to any decision. Perhaps nothing can impair our future more than our own ambivalence about what we want. Without a foundation, we are going along for the ride from site to site, letting others show us the interesting places but never arriving at a destination. Think about how much sense it would make to call a taxi and not give the driver an address or, worse yet, let him determine the destination for us. Why do we do this with our own life? With our team or organization?

Samir understood that I might wonder about the sites I missed on our tour and might blame him if I did not like what he chose for me. Thus, he left the decision up to me. He even used the word "responsibility" when referring to my task of telling him where to go. It was my duty, my obligation, to choose for myself. I was ultimately accountable for the decision, not Samir.

I did not know where I wanted to go in Cairo because I was in unfamiliar territory, which obscured my sense of direction, and thinking about the future puts us in "new territory." In spite of these elements of newness, we must articulate a destination in order to move forward. What do we want our future to look like? Where and when do we want to arrive? If we don't have answers to these questions, we need to work on discovering them.

Complete the following statements. Your answers should contain sufficient detail and a clear direction of where you want to go, what you want to become, or what you want to pursue. Your desired "destination" should be challenging but attainable.

I am most energized when...
I am passionate about...
I derive joy from...
I value...
It is amazing that I get paid for...
I wish I could get paid for...
My favorite place is...
For fun, I...
I am most proud of...
I wish I could...
If given an opportunity, I would...
I have always dreamed of...
I am good at...
Someday I would like to...
If I could do it again, I would...

These statements are not for public display. They are your contract with yourself, serving as a source of inspiration and energy, a rallying point. The answers will help you refine what you want.

Articulating what you want is a prerequisite to everything that follows—the use of tools, plans, methods, strategies, coaches, mentors, and tour guides. As Samir suggested, only after we figure out what we "wish" for can we determine the best route for getting there.

Maxim: We cannot outsource our intent. No one can decide for us what we truly want. This discovery cannot be delegated.

Compilation of Desire Phase Questions

- What are you inspired by? Why?
- Who inspires you the most?
- What kind of people do you like to be surrounded by? Why?
- What makes you feel productive?
- What makes you feel that time is flying by?
- When was the last time you experienced happiness? What were you doing?
- What makes you feel proud of yourself?
- What makes you feel proud of your team or your company?
- What would you do if not limited by the need for money?
- What commitment or initiative have you been postponing? How does procrastination make you feel?
- What intrigues you?
- What would you like to know more about?
- What is the one thing you would like to accomplish before you die?
- What activities do you enjoy the most?
- What kind of work would you do for free?
- Do you chronically feel tired at the end of each workday?
- What is your "picture" of happiness?
- What is your "picture" of success?
- What gives you a deep sense of satisfaction? Accomplishment?
- What is your "gift"? How are you using it?
- What work or activity do you find most rewarding?
- What contributions or achievements do you find most desirable?

- What issues or causes are you most moved by?

- Which world problem or challenge would you like to see solved?

- How would you like to serve others if time were abundant?

- What would you like to become?

- What would you like to achieve?

- What would you like to express?

- How would you like that picture to look?

- What impact would you like to have on others?

- What will truly fulfill your aspirations?

- What would you like your legacy to be?

- I am most energized when...

- I am passionate about...

- I derive joy from...

- I value...

- It is amazing that I get paid for...

- I wish I could get paid for...

- My favorite place is...

- For fun, I...

- I am most proud of...

- I wish I could...

- If given an opportunity, I would...

- I have always dreamt of...

- I am good at...

- Someday I would like to...

- If I could do it again, I would...

Design

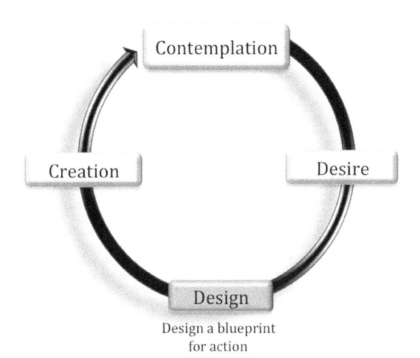

Design a blueprint
for action

Chapter 11

Planning Backward to Move Ahead

Good ideas are shot down by people who assume that the future is merely an extension of the past.

—Joel Barker, Futurist

Our conception of the future shapes how we act and behave in the present, which, in the end, will profoundly affect the way we lead, the way we plan for the future, and the way we live. How do you deal with time and with change?

1. Do you find yourself anchored to the past, controlling and preserving things the way they are today because you dread the uncertainties of tomorrow?

2. Do you find yourself in crisis mode, resisting change because you fear where it may take you?

3. Do you find yourself anticipating a future that seems inevitable?

4. Do you find yourself creating the future that you want?

Depending on our conception of the future, we consciously or unconsciously embrace a certain type of planning mode or style. We do this to protect ourselves from a change that appears threatening (e.g., a realignment of job responsibilities) or to open ourselves up to an opportunity that looks appealing (e.g., a job overseas or a promotion).

There are three traditional modes of planning: *reactive, inactive,* and *preactive.* Think of a wave in the ocean as a metaphor for change. When *reactive planners* see a big wave, they try to swim against the current. They do not want to be dragged down, so they take action to ensure that they swim to a safer place (the known past) where the waves are not as threatening. *Inactive planners* try to anchor themselves where they are by going under the water or jumping and letting the waves go by. They reemerge in the same spot they were and remain active by jumping or submerging themselves to guard against future waves that threaten their position. *Preactive planners* do not swim against the current, but they do not stay put. They use the momentum of the waves to surf to safety, to follow current trends and join the bandwagon of popular practices.

The diagrams that follow illustrate these planning styles and their implications. The lower line represents time. The past is to the left, the present is toward the center, and the future is to the right. We are continuously moving out of the past and into the future. The upper line represents where we want to be.

Reactive planners romanticize the past. They would rather be where they once were than where they are now. They are motivated by the overriding belief that things were better as they were before. They prefer "the good old days" and look to the past for inspiration. They rely on experience and adopt familiar solutions to problems. They are most comfortable with things they've seen in the past and with retro-thinking to revitalize the way it was. Their plan consists of how to get from where they are to where they once were (reestablishment of the past).[1]

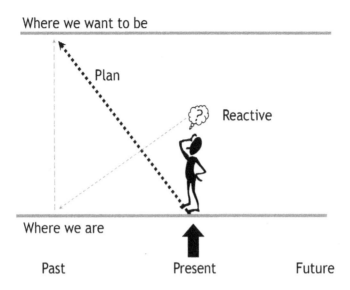

Figure 1. Reactive planning (Ackoff 1999).

People will not admit that they are trying to move backward, but their actions tell the tale. When reactive people are confronted with problems, they concentrate on identifying the source. If you can remove the source, so goes the logic, and you can return to where you were yesterday. As a nation, we use this approach to address large social issues. Prohibition is an example of how this kind of thinking can backfire.

In the 1920s, the major social problem in the United States was alcoholism. As a nation, we looked at the problem and asked what is the cause of alcoholism? Our answer, alcohol. The plan was to look back and find out when we did not have these problems. So the plan was to remove the cause and do away with alcohol. Prohibition didn't get rid of the problem; in fact it created a bigger one. Organized crime took hold. [1]

If we expect to get the most desirable outcomes from how we plan, we need to abandon a reactionary response to problems. There is something fundamentally wrong with reactive thinking. We seek out what is wrong and remove it. We identify what we do not want, and we try to eliminate it in the mistaken belief that we will be better off. It doesn't happen that way. In most cases, we are left with something worse. Eliminating what we do not want will not guarantee that we will get what we want, but we behave as if it would.

Several summers ago while vacationing on the Eastern Seaboard, I took the family to dine out. My children asked the age-old question, "Where are we going?"

"It is a surprise," I said.

The children began to see a dreaded theme emerging—fish! All the signs on the road pointed to a future that they did not want. My son took charge and communicated his concern through a question. "Dad, you know that we do not like fish, right?"

"I know. Do not worry about it, because we are not having fish tonight. We are going to have liver, the best liver in town!"

They all reacted in disgust, because they hated liver more than they hated fish. By eliminating what they did not want, they were getting something worse. Moreover, they were not getting what they really wanted: pizza! It was a trick on my part, but it proved a point. Our actions must be aimed at getting what we *do* want, not at getting rid of what we do not want.

Focusing our efforts on what we want is central to the second step of the CDDC cycle: discovering what we truly *desire*. Eliminating or avoiding an undesirable condition—such as a job problem or an interpersonal dynamic—does not ensure that we will attain what we desire.

We can't assume that if we eliminate what we do not want, our future will be better. It could be worse. We must take this important principle into account when we shape our future. Conscious avoidance of failure channels our energies toward getting rid of what we do not want. This reactive approach not only prevents us from achieving desired outcomes, but it accelerates what we dread most: failure, pain, and other negative repercussions. We must focus on getting what we want, pursuing our aspirations.

We cannot lead effectively if we are overly concerned with failure. Toxic thoughts will push our mental and physical efforts in the wrong direction, and we ultimately become defensive and self-protective.

Good golfers understand this principle. They're in the middle of the fairway. They have the hole in sight. They begin there and work back to where they are standing until they find a spot in front of them aligned with the pin. They calculate the distance and consider the wind direction, but they ignore the water, sand hazards, and out-of-bound markers. To acknowledge them is to allow negative thoughts to intrude on their image of where they want to be: on the green, close to the pin.

Professional racecar drivers apply this principle in critical situations. If they lose control of the car, they focus on where they want to steer the car instead of looking at where the car is heading.

A Leader of One recognizes that our tendency to avoid failure inhibits our ability to engage in activities that lead to success. Success requires that we focus on success, not on the avoidance of failure.

Inactive planners are those people who apparently are where they want to be. Notice how the lines at the top and bottom of the earlier diagram frame it, and notice now how those lines merge in the next diagram. Inactive planners love the moment and are validated in their thinking by keeping busy. They are represented as upside down, because they are dealing with crises and anything else that threatens the status quo. If they are busy, they think they are keeping things the way they want. They are active in the moment but passive about what's ahead.

Inactive planners take a stance against change that sounds pragmatic and reasonable. They pretend to accept change but contend that the proposals under consideration are flawed. In response to any deviation from the status quo, they will tell you that they've "seen it all," that "these problems are different," or "we tried that years ago, and it didn't work."

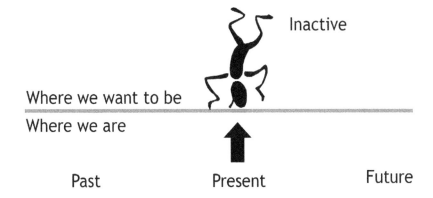

Figure 2. Inactive planning (Ackoff 1999).

Their opposition to change is based on self-interest. To an inactive planner, new ideas are primarily intellectual novelties that they must influence so that they never become a threat to their security. They see change as disruptive and even wrenching, and they believe that any change from the present course may ultimately do more harm than good.

Preactive planners forecast what is going to happen five or ten years out. Their mode of operation is to predict and formulate where they want to be in that world and then frame it as a vision. The main problem with this approach lies with forecasting. Forecasting strives to describe and know what cannot be known (the future). Moreover, if the forecasting of the future is off target, the plan becomes worthless.

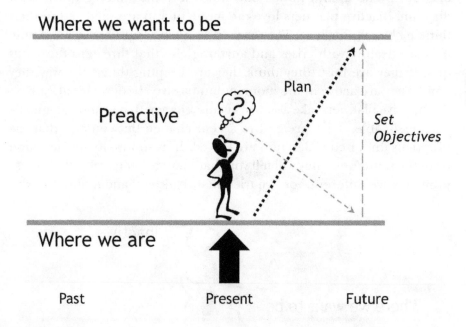

Figure 3. Preactive planning (Ackoff 1999).

Conventional wisdom holds that to understand the future, we need to study the past. The study of the past is not only beneficial but essential to understanding what lies ahead. Even though trying to predict the future is a fascination for many scholars, historians still outnumber futurists, and colleges and libraries focus more attention on "what was" than on what "may be" in the future.

The fourth planning style is less traditional. *Interactive planners* have a conception of the future that acknowledges that the future can go in any direction. They recognize that prediction can bring little value to the discussion of the future. They build upon an idea popularized by physicist Eric Hoffer: "The only way to predict the future is to have the power to shape the future." [2] This view reinforces the notion that we can design and create our path to the future.

Interactive planning, a practice developed at Dow Labs in the late 1950s, is a completely different way of planning. You do not use the present to plan for the future but use the future to plan for the present. In other words, you plan backward! This planning style is ideally suited to our purposes. Only when we recognize our potential to shape the future can we become empowered to create it.

Interactive planners formulate where they want to be through dream and design. What happens between now and "then" (the future) depends on what they *do* between now and then. Because they can't shape the future in the future, their only option is to take action in the present.

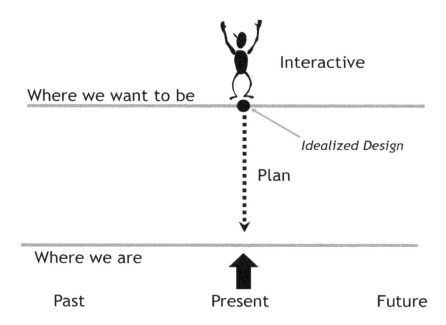

Figure 4. Interactive planning (Ackoff 1999).

According to interactive planners, it is better to plan from a desired destination or endpoint *back* to the current location or situation. By doing so, the concept of feasibility is enhanced, and the speed of attainment is increased.

The benefits of backward planning were discovered in the 1950s by applied mathematician Richard Bellman, and he called the process *dynamic programming*.[3] The interesting thing about the principle is that most kids know it intuitively, but as adults, we lose that perspective. Kids will solve a maze puzzle, for example, by starting at the exit and backtracking to the entrance because it is simpler. The rationale for this process is not obvious. The proof is complicated, involving functional analysis and advanced calculus, which goes beyond the scope of this book. However, the following example, courtesy of Russ Ackoff, illustrates the point.

If you are familiar with the scoring method for tennis, you can figure out how many matches must be played in a sixty-four-player tournament to select one winner. The tournament is single elimination—that is, "win or go home." Take a piece of paper and spend a few minutes trying to come up with the answer. Again, the question is, "How many matches are played in a sixty-four-player tournament in order to select one winner?"

You probably figured out that the answer is sixty-three. The problem is not getting there but how you did it. You probably envisioned sixty-four players in a bracket system vying against one another, with thirty-two winners as the result. They in turn played against one another, resulting in sixteen winners, then eight, then four, then two, and then one. The problem is that the process took longer than it should have and involved way too much math.

That is how most planning is done. People will say, "We are here at sixty-four and we want to be at one. How do we get there?" They develop tactics to accomplish short-term goals (thirty-two), midrange goals (sixteen), and long-range ones (eight, four, and two). This is way too busy, and, as we move forward in time, the plan becomes dated because of changes in the environment. The tendency is to abandon the plan.

The better and faster way to get to your desired destination is dynamic programming. If you *start* at your desired state, you will get there faster and more easily. One way to do it is to change the question. Instead of asking how to get "from here to there," ask how to get "from there to here." If the tournament has sixty-four players, how many losers do we need to get to one champion? Now you see it: sixty-three. No division needed![4]

The time to get to your desired state is greatly reduced. That is what all this book is about: inventing ways to get to the desired future faster. Let me change the numbers and ask you the same question. Say that the tournament has 884 players. How many losers do we need? See the difference? It took you a split second to say 883! The future belongs to those who ask the right questions and find the way to get there faster.

We can apply this mindset to any situation involving the future. We could be in the throes of a job search, deciding which college to go to, or buying a house. Even in those scenarios, we can apply the notion of backward planning. We begin by dreaming of and designing the ideal, and then we search for what is closest to it. Let's say that we want to buy a house. We envision the ideal requirements and specifications—ranch style, with a view of the lake, country kitchen, three miles from town, no older than thirty years, etc. Our decision will be simplified when we search based on what is closest to the ideal.

As we work from an ideal future to the present, our concept of what is feasible changes. We realize that the most effective way to create the future is by continuously approximating or closing the gap between the ideal and the present. For this reason, we must contemplate and dream first! Not knowing what we want ideally is like practicing at a shooting range without a target. Our bullets could end up anywhere.

Exploration of the future is similar to the exploration of the past. Because neither the future nor the past exists in the present, we must use inferential reasoning to know either one of them. If we start from where we are and look into the future, we see obstructions—laws, regulations, the culture, the environment, "them," or something outside of ourselves that can deter our success. The reality is that we are the primary barrier, and our mindset is the greatest impediment. If we start from the future we want, we see possibilities, opportunities, and hope.

Planning backward strengthens and deepens our desire, and it refines our capacity to design. The process will never be perfect; it will never be complete, because it is dynamic, ongoing, never ending.

Maxim: Do not react to the present you dislike, but interact with the future you want. It is better to plan for yourself, no matter how badly, than to be planned for, no matter how well. Strive for that which you consider ideal. Even if you never attain it, you will end up in a better place.

Chapter 12

Leveraging Your Perspective for Enduring Change

> *In one way or another, we are forced to deal with complexities, with "wholes" or "systems" in all fields of knowledge. This implies a basic reorientation in scientific thinking.*

—Ludwig von Bertalanfy, Systems Theorist

Committing to your purpose and sustaining that effort require discipline. Change is difficult, and a relapse to a previous state is always tempting. A friend of mine told me, "There is no neutral in life. You either move forward or you move back." Doing nothing does not maintain the status quo. Inaction takes us backward, taking us farther from our goals.

Trying to create change is like trying to get in shape. It takes many months to develop stamina and endurance but only a few weeks to lose it all. This scenario often plays out when we are trying to develop the positive habits associated with sustainable change.

For change to be enduring, we must address it from multiple perspectives, from three worldviews or domains: the *physical,* the *emotional,*
and the *logical.* [1]

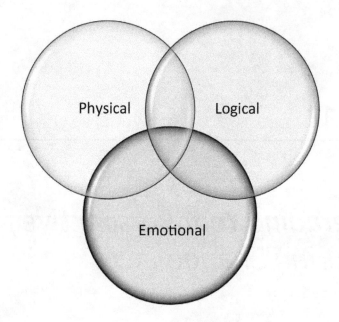

Figure 5. Physical, emotional, and logical model (Scherkenbach, W. W.
1991).

Our ability to change will be incomplete and ineffective if we neglect any one domain. When shaping the future, we must integrate these
worlds to create meaningful and enduring impact. Let's take a look at
each one as we explore a common example of a human activity: dieting.

Physical

The physical world is the most tangible aspect of change. If we commit to the goal of losing weight, our physical world orientation will influence our strategy. Our strategy will probably be driven by how we look.
We engage in rigorous exercise over a period of time. Running, swim-
ming, weightlifting, and other strenuous activities will be in alignment
with this perspective. Our feedback mechanism will be visible and tangible. We look at ourselves in the mirror, step on the scale, and measure

our body parts. We notice how loose our clothes are becoming. We measure body fat and keep detailed records. From this perspective, the thinner we look, the better.

The physical world is one of structures, mockups, blueprints, prototypes, and test runs. This world is experiential and associated with learning by doing. People who lean toward a physical view of the world place their faith in numbers, data, and quantifiable, verifiable evidence. They are often drawn to careers as engineers, builders, orthodontists, architects, and graphic designers. They believe that "if you cannot measure it, you cannot manage it."

"Not so fast," say people who represent the other worldviews, the emotional and the logical. To them, most of the important attributes that one needs to succeed defy measurement. How can we measure doubt or intuition? Indeed, intuition is often defined as our ability to make good decisions in the absence of data, and how would we measure passion or desire or sacrifice? These attributes are elusive and intangible but equally important to success.

Think about a person who has influenced your life. It could be a family member, friend, teacher, coach, mentor, spiritual leader, or world leader. Recall a meaningful interaction with that person. Why did that person make an impact on you? What was special? What imprint did he or she leave on you? Write down five characteristics or attributes associated with that person.

You probably do not have a list of quantitative measures or precise descriptions. You probably said that the person "inspired me," "believed in me," "listened to me," "trusted me," or "led by example." These are desirable characteristics, but they don't belong in the physical world. They are best understood in an emotional context.

I suggest that even the most basic measures to preserve objectivity are influenced by perception and interpretation. The forces of subjectivity will fight relentlessly to prevail.

Imagine this scenario. Two college graduates apply for the same job at the same company. When the recruiter comes to the campus, she thinks that there is a mistake in the file because it appears as if she has duplicates. Both files are identical. They showcase two graduates from the same institution, both of whom double-majored in finance and accounting. Upon further review, she notes that both live at the same address, both are citizens of the United States, both are born on the same date, and they have the same last name. Indeed, an error, she thinks! Looking once again, she notices a difference in the first names.

The recruiter is intrigued by this situation and goes to the reception area where she recognizes the subjects because of their strikingly identical physical appearance. The recruiter greets them and jumps to a conclusion. "How wonderful," she says. "I did not know that you were twins!"

The students look at each other and laugh. One replies, "We are not twins."

The evidence in their files is so strong and convincing that the recruiter insists, "Oh, come on, you have to be twins!"

The students look at each other, and one says, "We come from a set of triplets!"

The data in the physical world was vast, accurate, verifiable, explicit, and visible, but the recruiter's thinking was flawed. It was incomplete because she did not entertain all of the possibilities that could have explained the situation. The evidence was objective, and yet subjective judgment prevailed! If the three domains—the physical, the emotional, and the logical—are not taken as a whole, each by itself will not yield a relevant and enduring outcome.

Emotional

The emotional domain is complex, because emotions are personal. They are difficult to isolate and study in their pure states. There is not a definitive taxonomy of emotions. Theories about emotion continue to evolve as a focus of vigorous interest in most branches of cognitive science. The constellation of emotions that a person experiences may also happen at an unconscious level, making this domain even more difficult to understand. Emotions fluctuate in intensity over time. Some are short lived and driven by the situation, while others, such as love, can be pervasive and enduring.

The word "emotion" is used to denote subjective feelings such as fear, anger, aversion, courage, dejection, desire, despair, envy, hate, hope, love, happiness, interest, surprise, wonder, sorrow, and so on. These powerful feelings are also linked to physiological changes in our body that can be measured—an increase in pulse rate, a rise in body temperature, or a change in rate of breathing. Most, however, defy measurement and even logic. It is not uncommon for the same event or experience to trigger different emotional reactions in the same individual or for a person to experience a strong emotion without any apparent reason.

Let's look again at the dieting example but this time view it through the "prism" of the emotional domain. A strong emotional orientation will impact our strategy. In the physical domain, it is a matter of how we look. In the emotional domain, it is a matter of how we feel. We want to increase our self-esteem and confidence. We step on the scale to read a number, but we derive joy from experiencing the psychological boost that accompanies weight loss.

Emotions play a crucial role in our daily lives, influencing our quality of life and priorities, and impacting our interpersonal relationships and our perception of self. People whose worldview is predominantly emotional are drawn to fields such as psychology, counseling, executive coaching, human resources, and ministering. If the physical domain addresses the letter of the law, the emotional domain represents the "spirit" of the law.

Logical

People whose orientation favors the logical domain are drawn to science, hypotheses, theories, and research. They place their belief in scientific proof, probabilities, and formulas. They value intellectual rigor. Professionals whose perspective falls within the logical domain include computer scientists, physicians, physicists, mathematicians, and logicians. They pursue objectivity and truth. They are less tolerant of ambiguity.

A person on a diet whose perspective is predominantly logical will study the health benefits associated with being physically fit and at the appropriate weight. Research will precede any action. This person will study how metabolism works and learn about the interactions of the food groups. They will first consult with their doctor and study diet plans, selecting or customizing the one that seems most appropriate. Caloric intake and nutritional values will be taken into serious consideration. People with a strong logical orientation will not be driven by how they look or feel but by the medical benefits of cleansing their systems, adding years to their life, and enhancing their endurance, stamina, and performance.

Our primary domain influences how we process information and how well we assimilate it. An engineering student in my business class approached me one day to let me know that he was struggling with the content presented in the last few weeks. "This is too complex for me," he said.

I was truly surprised. He was a bright aerospace engineering student who was specializing in wing design. The course I was teaching covered basic statistical thinking and the application of statistics to monitor the variability of a process. He had done well in what was typically the most challenging aspect of the course. His struggles had to do with the importance of visioning, the value and process for creating constancy of purpose for a business, and the team process for developing a strategy to pursue that vision.

I could not relate to his struggles because, from my paradigm, visioning and strategy were a lot easier to understand than wing design. I asked him to elaborate.

"In engineering," he said, "the formulas are set. You design following rigorous methods and proven principles. If you run the data through the appropriate model, you can tell if the computerized wing design will work or not under the various tolerances and harsh environments that you test against."

He continued. "First, you define the requirements. They help you determine how strong the wing has to be in the most demanding conditions such as takeoff, landing, and steep turns. Second, you choose a structure type. You use historical information as a starting point to design the general shape and the internal structure, materials, and curvature. Third, you calculate the performance of your initial designs. After numerous tests, you build and test the prototype. In other words, at the end of the process, you will know with certainty if the plane will fly or not!"

"In business," he said, "it seems that 'it all depends.' You can develop a great plan, but it may not work because of 'culture.' People can resist the change, and they can sabotage ideas. In engineering, resistance can be measured, and you can compensate for it in the design. You can increase robustness in the system to ensure performance under the most strenuous conditions."

His struggle was over the fact that he was not sure if his business design would yield positive results. He had a strong logical nature. He was filtering subjective material through a logical lens, which was a constant challenge for him (and is for others who lean toward a physical worldview). The same is true for people with a strong emotional perspective. They do not relate well to what could be considered impersonal, scientific fact.

Integrating the Three Worlds

We've seen from the dieting example that a holistic blend is required if the results of dieting are to be enduring. When we integrate the three perspectives, we form a *system of knowledge.*

A *system* is a whole consisting of two or more parts that interact to accomplish an aim. [2] The system enables us to appreciate interactions necessary to initiate and sustain a desired change. If we do not see these worlds as a whole, a process (losing weight, for example) will not be as effective or as feasible. What good will it do to know and understand the benefits of being fit if we do not change our physical behavior? The opposite is also true. Starting a vigorous diet without the proper understanding of nutritional balance may lead to malnutrition.

The physical, emotional, and logical worlds do not operate in isolation. They are not mutually exclusive. One cannot operate successfully in its purest form, independent of the other two. It is easier to understand them if we think of them as primary colors. Very seldom do we see them in their pure state, and variations and combinations produce other colors. Let's look at how the domains can blend.

The intersection between the logical and physical worlds leads to science. The dictionary defines science as "the intellectual and practical activity encompassing the systematic study of the structure and behavior of the physical and natural world through observation and experiment." [3] In its most basic sense, science focuses on the translation of learning from research and experimentation into practical applications in the real world.

The intersection of logic and emotion leads to psychology, a social science designed to study emotions in order to explain and modify behavior. Psychology is the science of mind, thought, and behavior.

The intersection between the physical domain and the emotional domain gives us art. Art is the external and physical manifestation of emotion. An artist brings emotions into the physical world through painting, sculpture, screenplays, etc.

The following questions will help you identify your dominant perspective. There are no right or wrong answers, and no domain is "better" than the others. Knowing what your dominant perspective is will help you become receptive to the others, a receptivity you will need as you seek enduring change.

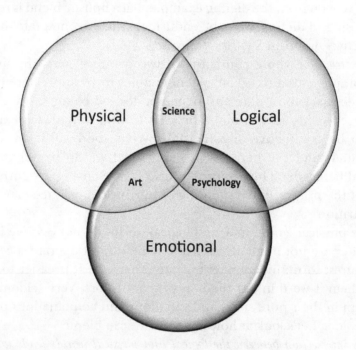

Figure 6. Expanded physical, emotional, and logical model.

Guiding Questions

Physical (*Relates to tangible, real-world action*)

1. By what methods are you executing your aim? Your desired future? The pursuit of your aspirations?

2. What is your definition of success?

3. How are you monitoring progress?

4. What metrics are important to you?

Logical (*Relates to the conceptualization, methodology, and design of an idea or course of action*)

1. Are your actions and decisions supported by theory, research, or best practices?

2. How do you ensure that this is a sound approach or plan?

3. Do you assess the potential for risks associated with your course of action?

4. Do you have a plan to mitigate failure?

Emotional (*Relates to the desire, passion, motivation, and inspiration of an idea or course of action*)

1. Are you sensitive to how your actions and behaviors are perceived by others?

2. What subjective indicators do you monitor to assess your progress?

3. Do you experience doubt or anxiety as you take action?

4. Do you typically experience confidence and optimism regarding your future? How is this reflected in your interactions?

The center of the model represents the critical intersection of the physical, emotional, and logical domains. Our efforts to shape our future must be anchored there if we wish for enduring change. A Leader of One recognizes that it is not about balance but about integration. Integration of our physical, emotional, and logical worlds will not guarantee success, but they are necessary components for achieving it.

Maxim: Shaping your future requires the integration of the three domains. In the intersection of the physical, emotional, and logical worlds, hope and wisdom meet.

Chapter 13

The Power of Design

Design must reflect the practical and aesthetic in business, but above all, good design must primarily serve people.

—Thomas J. Watson, Founder of IBM

The discovery and articulation of our desired future resemble the way a family goes about designing a house with an architect. The architect asks questions to help them envision the size and amenities and to get a feel for their needs and lifestyle. How many people will live in it? Where do they most like to gather? What activities do they engage in? Do they need a home office? Do they like to entertain? Do they host guests frequently? Do they own pets? Does anyone in the family have special requirements because of a medical condition or physical challenge? What is the budget? Architects design from a perspective of empathy, to ensure that their blueprint captures the needs and requirements of the family.

At the end of this stage, there is no house, just a concept on paper, yet this stage cannot be bypassed. What a mistake it would be to break ground and hurry construction, and what a tragedy to move into the house and realize that it doesn't meet the family's needs.

As we design our future, we play the roles of both architect and family member. As the architect, the job is to translate our desires into a "blueprint" that will serve as the basis for building our future. In this role, it is our job to make changes to it in such a way that we can enhance the house—our future—as a whole.

Asking the right questions and answering them thoughtfully is critical to the design phase. The questions may be unsettling to answer and the answers may be difficult to formulate, because we are starting from a point of possibilities rather than certainties. Answering certain fundamental questions gives us a chance to refine what we want.

Your design should be the outcome of reflection and visioning. Ask yourself, "What do I really want, and why? How do I know? What will I do if I achieve it?"

Just as architects work to improve the house as a whole, we must stay sensitive to improving our life as a whole. One powerful and effective way to go about this process is to think in terms of your *ideal future* and to adopt a method tested and proven in the design of complex systems: those in businesses, schools, stores, and hospitals, even in the design of technical and mechanical systems such as computers and cars. This method is called *idealized design.* [1]

The idealized design process requires that you "pick up the brush" and paint your own canvas. It begins with the assumption that you have a clean slate, your past has dissolved, your problems have vanished, your organization is destroyed, and your challenges are eliminated, but the environment in which you work or live is the same. For example, you would still live in the twenty-first century, be born into the same family, be your same age, and so on. You ask yourself, "If I were to create anything that I wanted, what would I like it to be?"

Whatever you come up with cannot be utopian. Your future will never be perfect, because life never is, so it must be subject to refinements. It must also be feasible, capable of being implemented now if you choose to pursue it.

This exercise offers an interlude to our future. It offers a mental space where we can exploit our imagination. Ideation and imagination are freeing and fun, but we may find that the present is not agreeable and may not cooperate with us. For this reason, we must take the actions and initiatives that shape our reality, not merely react to them. Uncertainty about the future is a stubborn reality, but trying to anticipate what will happen is not the answer. Predicting the future, no matter how well, will never influence it. [2]

Here are some practical guidelines for using idealized design to shape the future. Review the chapter "Leveraging Your Perspective for Enduring Change" so that you are familiar again with the three domains: the physical, emotional, and the logical. Find a quiet place where you will not be interrupted for a reasonable time. Do not bring any gadgets that may distract you. Just bring a pad of paper and a pencil, and ask yourself, "If I were to create my ideal future with anything that I wanted, what would I like it to be?"

Think of your life in terms of the three domains. Ideate whom you wish to become—skills, dexterity, abilities, intellectual depth and development, relationships, spirituality, wealth, health, and sense of happiness and joy that you would like possess and develop. You can start anywhere. You can move freely from one domain to another as you develop your answer. Let the process flow. Reflect.

As soon as you have identified a trait of your idealized future, stop and document it. Briefly explain why this feature is desirable, even if it is obvious. Explore how this will help you move closer to your desired future and move on to developing the next feature. Be courageous! Build your answer around your "gift," your desire, your hope and do not pass judgment on what you are writing. You cannot go wrong if you are designing what you authentically desire.

Ensure that whatever you come up with is technologically feasible, and economically and socially viable. You must be able to adopt it if you decide to pursue it. Do not reject or embrace anything too early. Ideas that appear to be incompatible or seem unattainable are okay, just document them and move on. Use "what if", "wouldn't it be nice if", and other conditional language. You are dealing with possibilities, not certainties. Think about how your future would look like if you had no excuses and no one to blame for your present or your past. Unleash yourself from the way things are and imagine how they could be.

Do not rush the creative process, let it simmer, reflect and build on it. The creative process is exploratory and divergent. Once you have developed enough content, converge and organize your ideas into a cohesive whole. This document will become your statement of purpose and the blueprint for action. Think of it as the prototype of your future.

Once you complete the idealization of your future, you must commit to action with resolve. Your actions to close the gap between the desired reality and the present one are the catalyst to shape your future. The realization phase begins with this commitment to action, using interactive planning. Idealization without realization is a mere fantasy. The idealization phase is creative and the realization phase is pragmatic. The realization phase requires you to determine a course of action, identify priorities, and determine the initial resources that you would need. Take the plunge into the realization, you will not have everything that you need as you get started but starting from where you are will allow you to gain momentum and discover or invent new pathways to your future.

Most of the realization obstructions are self-imposed psychological barriers. Believing that "this will not work," or "that it is too complicated, simplistic, or utopian," will lead to abandonment. Start with the conviction that what you want to create is attainable and you will be surprised by how many of the elements of your idealized design can be accomplished as you explore their realization. Mobilizing your future from concept into action is essential because there is no other way to pursue your desired results.

Idealized design is a powerful framework for influencing the future. Its methodology is applicable at both the personal and organizational levels.

I spearheaded an idealized design process in arguably the most complex organization in the world, the White House. We adopted the ideas espoused in this chapter at the White House Communications Agency (WHCA), the largest presidential support unit within the White House. WHCA is responsible for providing instantaneous telecommunications to support the president.

WHCA houses a workforce of about nine hundred highly skilled personnel from all the branches of the armed forces and the Coast Guard, as well as a handful of civilians from the Department of Defense. This team works around the clock and around the globe ensuring that the president has robust telecommunications capabilities to lead the nation effectively from any location and under any circumstances. These capabilities include video archiving of presidential events, manufacture and deployment of the lecterns, stage lights, sound systems, flags, tele-prompters, and encrypted voice, video, and data. Throughout each busy day in the Oval Office, onboard Marine One Helicopter, Air Force One, or in the presidential limousine, WHCA is there. If the president is visiting Africa and needs to connect with someone elsewhere in the world or wants to connect with the astronauts in the space lab, WHCA makes the connection.

The mission of the agency is critical, and thus the processes of person-nel selection and hiring are extremely rigorous in terms of background checks and assessments. There are no unimportant jobs in support of the president. Disconnecting the president from a time-sensitive nation-al security call or having the wrong speech in the teleprompter can cre-ate unspeakable havoc. The agency takes pride in the fact that only the best and the brightest are selected for presidential support.

If we hired only the best, we should have been the best organiza-tion. Why was it necessary to embark on an idealized design? It became evident that we had good people trapped in a reactive culture. We were so caught up in the present that we neglected our future. The agency de-veloped a short-term focus, and the process of CDDC seemed utopian, because we were in a day-to-day operational tempo.

It was difficult to establish strategic priorities in that environment. As a result, our leaders became tacticians, not strategists. The next move, as though in an arcade game, was important rather than the choice of the game itself. As a result, we lacked vision, direction, and focus. The results began to show in terms of performance and diminished quality of life at work. WHCA's erosion became evident when the presidential seal from the podium fell during one of President Clinton's speeches, when phone calls were disconnected, or when the teleprompter opera-tor struggled to keep up with the pace of the president.

Problems with phone calls or podiums were not the real issues. These were symptoms of the organizational malaise taking root. There were many other issues emerging in the organization, but we were all too busy working to address them. We were coping but feeling the pain of increased dysfunction.

I gained my boss's attention when I shared the findings of an or-ganizational climate survey that I had conducted. The results reflected low morale, poor dissemination of information, lack of vision, lack of planning, ineffective distribution of workload, outdated technology, lethargic procurement processes, and many other ailments. These issues formed a system of problems and depicted the full landscape of the mess. It would have been ineffective to try to address those issues in isolation, because the issues were interrelated. The intervention required a holistic approach.

By addressing the issues independently, we would be engaging in the organizational equivalent of the popular arcade game "Whack-A-Mole" in which you whack a mole only to see more moles emerging. The better you get at hitting one, the faster other moles come out.

When this happens, you are trapped in a cycle of dysfunction. Awareness of the interrelationship of problems is essential and a strong reason for adopting idealized design.

We had to change in fundamental ways in order to create a better organization and not simply address each symptom in isolation. I briefed the director of the WHCA, Col. Simmons, on the need for the transformative process of CDDC and the benefits of idealized design. He understood the importance of creating a collective sense of purpose, one that would help us bind as one team with one aim. He was receptive to the power of articulating and designing the future, but I could sense his hesitancy.

The truth was that our climate seemed inhospitable to an organization-wide redesign. The mission was in high gear, and the president was traveling all over the United States and the world. "We can't cripple our mission. The things you are suggesting require a massive effort. We can't ask the president to slow down just because we have to redesign," said Col. Simmons. He felt that we had to "change the tires on the car while in motion," and that seemed impossible. "We must press on with the mission. I see the need for it, and you've hit the issues on the head, but I'm concerned about the process to make this a reality."

How could we embrace change without threatening the existing mission or negatively affecting the relationships among the stakeholders—customers, suppliers, and employees? This is the challenge that we all face at the personal level. Our long-term purpose becomes blurred and obscured by day-to-day activities, routines, and crises. We feel that we can't stop today to create tomorrow, but we must find a way to sustain today while building tomorrow.

I pointed out to Col. Simmons that when the Department of Transportation was working on a new bridge, it didn't destroy the old one until the new one was finished. "That's how we'll do it," I said. "We will continue to perform the mission, and at the same time, we will have 'construction' going on. Our bridge will be a metaphorical one, constructed by all of our people. This participation will help rekindle our spirit of cooperation and renew our commitment to excellence and first-class presidential support. Most importantly, the process will institutionalize a participative environment and unleash the full creative, technical, and intellectual potential of our workforce as we chart a common future."

"This construction must take place while supporting our mission flawlessly. I rely on you to make this happen," he said.

I called a leadership meeting and presented a synopsis of the need to redesign WHCA and the key points of my conversation with the boss. Immediately, people began arguing about everything I said and voicing excuses: we do not have the time for this, this is good for corporations but not for us, our problems are unique, and so on.

I patiently addressed all their emotional reactions. At the end of the hour, they were skeptical but curious. "Dr. Suárez, why do you want to push for this comprehensive redesign?" This was a legitimate concern that required clarification before embarking on this journey.

No organization or individual is immune to change from positive or negative external pressures. Threats and opportunities can arise from anywhere. As the environment shifts, we have to respond to it. We can *react* to changing conditions in the environment, or we can take a *proactive* approach and use the power of *design* to create our desired conditions, our future.

Reacting to changes will distract and blindside us, narrowing our attention to the short term. Proactively addressing the issues will lead to a heightened level of awareness about the influence that we can have on our future.

We developed a list of questions to guide the discussions. These questions are useful to any leader or organization with plans to undergo a redesign. Beware: If you do not like the answers, the need for a redesign is highly likely.

- Are you dealing with the same problems you had a few years ago?

- Are you losing the people you want to keep and trapped with the people you want to lose?

- Are you fitting people to jobs or jobs to people?

- How do people find out what their jobs are?

- Are you having problems implementing your plans?

- Is your firing process better than your hiring process?

- Are you managing the actions of your subordinates and wondering why they don't do things according to your instructions?

- Are you uncertain about how to ensure learning and development within the organization?

- Do you feel that you could update your skills if only you had the time?

- Is the process by which you make policies a participative and effective one?

- Are people afraid of reporting and sharing their mistakes?

- Do you find people repeating the mistakes made by other organizations in your field?

- Do you have the data and information you need to make sound decisions?

- Are you aware of how the problems you solve create a ripple effect of problems in other areas of the organization?

- Are you having problems adapting to changes in the environment?

- Would you like to offer your people a better quality of life at work?

- Would you like to enhance opportunities for professional development?

- Have you ever asked your people what *you* can do to allow them to do their jobs better?

- Have you told your employees what *they* can do to allow you to do your job better?

- Do you know your customer's perception of your service or support?

We engaged in passionate yet candid dialogue about these and other issues that had great influence on our overall performance, strategic direction, and culture. Discussing these topics helped WHCA's leadership recognize the need to take action and ownership of the organization's destiny. We assumed that WHCA was destroyed—we had no equipment, no personnel, no policies, no facilities—but the need to provide telecommunications support to the presidency remained. What kind of agency would we create if we could create whatever we wanted (given that it was technologically feasible, socially viable, and not utopian)?

In this initial stage, it was vital to keep the scope of the effort in perspective. I emphasized that the Design phase was not about merely fixing what was wrong but about creating something fundamentally better than what we had. This was a "clean slate" effort.

We continued our discussions until we articulated what we wanted to create, although it was tentative and vague. Some broad themes emerged. We wanted to improve organizational planning, increase organizational flexibility, increase organizational and individual learning, improve decision making, increase cooperation and teamwork, enhance the quality of life at work, and have timely, relevant, accurate information and communication to help us perform our mission with distinction. These sounded more like a wish list, and wishes are not a strategy.

We developed a comprehensive design containing the specific details of what we wanted to accomplish along with the necessary policies, resources, implementation priorities, and commitment to make the design a reality. We published and disseminated a publication called *An Idealized Redesign of the White House Communications Agency,* [3] but at that stage, no changes had been made to the organization.

At the end of the idealized design process, you will have nothing tangible. There is no "house," just a concept on paper, but this process is essential, foundational to everything else. There are no shortcuts. The document is the manifesto. The future does not respond to documents but to action, yet we cannot rush to action without knowing what we want and where we are going.

Unfortunately, that is exactly how many of us live our lives and lead organizations—tearing off to the next event, the next appointment, the next initiative, addicted to the rush of attending to urgent matters and moving fast to nowhere.

It seems paradoxical, but as you develop your idealized future, it is critical to think in terms of the present. The reason is simple, yet the implications are far-reaching. Russ Ackoff, who contributed much to the widespread practice of idealized design, reminds you that "if you don't know what you would do right now, you cannot possibly know what you would want to do in fifteen or twenty years." [4]

A design of the future depends on a forecast of the future, but forecasting becomes less effective as the rate of change increases in our surroundings. The variables are so many and the uncertainties so great that it would be foolish to pretend that we can plan our life with high confidence today based on what might happen far in the future. We have no choice but to make assumptions about our future. Many mistakenly believe that an assumption is nothing but a forecast in disguise. Not so.

Russ Ackoff helped me appreciate the difference. He asked me, "Do you own a car?"

"Yes," I said.

"Do you have a spare tire in your car?"

"Yes."

"Why?"

I did not know what he was driving at, but he continued. "Is that because you are going to forecast when you will have a flat tire the next time you go out? In fact, your forecast is that you are not going to have a flat tire, so why do you carry a spare tire?"

We do so because we *assume* a flat tire is possible, not because we *forecast* that one is going to happen. This is based on possibility, not probability. An *assumption* is about *possibility*, and a *forecast* is about *probability*.

We have to make assumptions about the future we want. We must address each one as if it will come true. With explicit assumptions, we can develop a plan that is robust, a way to move from design to the last stage of the cycle, Creation.

The idealized design of the WHCA proved to be a catalyst to mobilize and posture the organization for the challenges of a new century.[5] We created a more flexible organizational design, increased and improved the interactions between functions, empowered people at each level by adopting a participative management style, revamped our training programs, reconfigured mission support to the president, developed a vibrant vision, and reallocated resources in pursuit of that vision.[6] It was not perfect or easy, designing a new organization and implementing the changes never is. Our design was subject to further adaptation based on our learning and on the fact that no environment is static.

In part, the success of WHCA's redesign enabled Col. Simmons to become the deputy assistant to the president and director of the White House military office. The Honorable Joseph J. Simmons IV had seen the power of design. He brought me with him, and we did it again! We began an idealized design of the White House Military Office with twenty-two hundred personnel ranging from those at Camp David to those on Air Force One. We did it again at the executive management and administration offices of the president.[7] These concepts work in complex organizations like the White House, they work in corporations and in academia, and they will work for you.

Idealized design helps us discover new possibilities and offers a powerful impetus for action. Design fuels our imagination, encouraging us to create in the present the future we want to have. Following the idealized design framework in this chapter will help you complete the first iteration of your blueprint. Revisit and revise it as you learn more about who you are, what you want to create, and where you want to go. You now have the template with which you can build and approximate the future you want. This process is dynamic and subject to adaptations as you move forward.

I strongly encourage you to develop your idealized design. You will be surprised by its power.

Maxim: Idealized design will ignite the creation of a better future. It will guide you in translating an intangible dream into a tangible reality.

Compilation of Design Phase Questions

- Do you find yourself anchored to the past, controlling and preserving things the way they are today because you dread the uncertainties of tomorrow?

- Do you find yourself in crisis mode, resisting change because you fear where it may take you?

- Do you live your life anticipating a future that seems to be inevitable?

- Do you live your life creating the future that you want?

- By what methods are you executing your aims? Your desired future? The pursuit of your aspirations?

- What is your definition of success?

- How are you monitoring progress?

- What metrics are important to you?

- Are your actions and decisions supported by theory, research, or best practices?

- How do you ensure that this is a sound approach or plan?

- Do you assess the potential for risks associated with your course of action?

- Do you have a plan to mitigate failure?

- Are you sensitive about how your actions and behaviors are perceived by others?

- What subjective indicators do you monitor to assess progress?

- Do you experience doubt or anxiety as you take action?

- Do you typically experience confidence and optimism regarding your future? How is this reflected in your interactions?

- Are you dealing with the same problems you had a few years ago?

- Are you losing the people you want to keep and trapped with the people you want to lose?

- Are you fitting people to jobs or jobs to people?

- How do people find out what their jobs are?

- Are you having problems implementing your plans?

- Is your firing process better than your hiring process?

- Are you managing the actions of your subordinates and wondering why they don't do things according to your instructions?

- Are you uncertain about how to ensure learning and development within the organization?

- Do you feel that you could update your skills if only you had the time?

- Is the process by which you make policies a participative and effective one?

- Are people afraid of reporting and sharing their mistakes?

- Do you find people repeating the mistakes made by other organizations in your field?

- Do you have the data and information you need to make sound decisions?

- Are you aware of how the problems you solve create a ripple effect of problems in other areas of the organization?

- Are you having problems adapting to changes in the environment?

- Would you like to offer your people a better quality of life at work?

- Would you like to enhance opportunities for professional development?

- Have you ever asked your people what *you* can do to allow them to do their jobs better?

- Have you told your employees what *they* can do to allow you to do your job better?

- Do you know your customer's perception of your service or support?

Phase 4

Creation

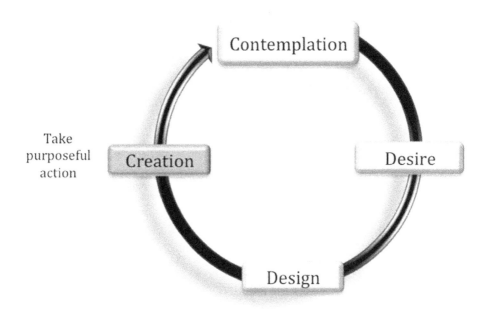

Chapter 14

Are We There Yet?

Every new beginning comes from some other beginning's end.

—Seneca, Roman Philosopher

We are entering the Creation phase of the CDDC cycle. This is where we migrate from blueprint to breaking ground, from vision to reality. In this phase, we must commit to building a pathway to our future. We may experience ambiguity, uncertainty, and doubt, yet we must press on. Our vision must prevail; our future can't wait.

Matt was one of the smartest students I've had. He was introspective and reflective in nature. His thinking seemed to be ahead of everyone else's, which created frustration when he was participating in a group setting. Blending in with others in a social event was a chore. Chit chat was not his forte. He was in a zone of his own, interacting socially only because he knew, at an intellectual level, that it was important to do so. He was a humble, unassuming individual with incredible potential and a great passion to give back to others.

He was quiet in class but always attentive. He saved most of his questions for casual moments before or after class. He typically sat in the back. He was not shy and could be outspoken when the issue deserved someone to step up to address it. He was a leader among his classmates and always led by example. He exerted influence on proceedings but could make others feel as if they were doing it all themselves. What a joy it was to have him in class.

I closed out the semester with a lecture about the power of vision and the importance of shaping our future. More than a lecture, it was a challenge, perhaps even an imperative. I finished class early because I had an important meeting in my office and also because university policy requires that we leave the room while students fill out the end-of-semester course evaluation.

As I rushed to my office, I heard footsteps and someone calling my name. I turned around and saw Matt. "Dr. Suárez, I have one more question," he said.

"Matt, I'm really in a hurry."

"It's just a minute!"

"Go ahead then, but please keep walking with me."

He popped the question, the big one lurking in the back of everyone's mind as they propelled themselves to the future. "How do you know if you've arrived?"

I naively thought, *Arrive?* "Arrive to my office? Follow me!"

"No, to the future. How do you know if you're there?"

I paused. "You want me to give you an answer right now? In a minute?"

It is a fascinating question and central to the conversation about shaping the future. The future is not a place. It is a concept, a notion that can exist only in our imagination. I asked Matt to tell me more.

He told me that when he was in high school, admission to college was his future. Once he was in college, joining the honors program was his future. As soon as he was selected to the honors program, graduation was his future, and then he wanted to work at a consulting firm. "I'm sure that when I start working, I will be designing something else in my mind about what I want to do next. I would like to start a foundation or something related to helping others enhance their education. So is there an end to this?"

This question was setting the stage for a deeper level of inquiry that had interesting implications. If there is no end to this chase, why should we pursue it? It seems irrational to go to such an elusive place if we never arrive.

Time is one of the few resources that we cannot save or accumulate. One cannot keep time in a bottle or a bank account. One cannot "save" leftover time. We can measure it and track its chronology, but it will go by regardless of what we do. For this reason, shaping the future requires that we invest our time wisely.

My colleague, Joel Barker, has a simple exercise that helps us understand this point. Extend your arm about six inches forward. Now try reaching back six inches. Your movement is visible, explicit, and feels real. Now try to reach forward six *seconds* and then reaching back six seconds. Is it possible? Can others see it?

Reaching back in time requires that we recreate and remember. Reaching forward demands that we create, that we imagine how the next few seconds, hours, days, or years will be. You can resist, stand motionless, and do nothing, but time will pass by anyway and quickly become part of your past.

Happiness has the same elusive quality. We cannot stockpile it. If we have a run of ten happy days, we cannot save them in case we face ten miserable days in the future. When our founding fathers were drafting the Declaration of Independence, they proclaimed that we were endowed with certain inalienable rights that included the pursuit of happiness. Just like the future, happiness is not a destination. Happiness is situational. It is rarely if ever, a fully completed experience. It exists within us, not outside of ourselves.

If we can never "attain" happiness or "arrive" at the future, why bother at all? Think back to the chapter "Who's Painting Your Canvas?" If you chose to be an artist rather than a critic, you chose to define your future rather have others do it for you. Ergo, we must forever be in pursuit of our future if we wish to take full control of our lives. Focusing on the future channels our thinking and helps us realize our ultimate purpose. We become empowered.

This process of exploring and defining our destination and planning for it is invaluable. When I was a child, I helped my mother plan our first real family vacation. I was involved in every step: selecting the destination, making reservations, looking at maps, picking up the airline tickets, coordinating tours, and buying clothes. All this activity became as exciting as the destination itself. We had fun in Florida, but after many years, I still recall that the greater value was in the planning and preparation. The anticipation was incredibly energizing, the lessons enduring.

Similarly in life, we must articulate our destination, put it into words. How we get there is life itself, so we must appreciate every step along the way. Consider your destination your magnet, your motivational draw. Do not get discouraged because the process seems long and hard. You may not get there, but that is never a reason to abandon the pursuit.

Pursuing our desires with discipline is more valuable than arriving at our destination. The irony is that when we think that we have arrived, we begin to decline, become complacent, or lose interest. Professional basketball player Michael Jordan (who won six National Basketball Association championships with the Chicago Bulls) and Swiss tennis extraordinaire Roger Federer (who has won an unprecedented seventeen majors) never let down because they arrived at the top. They continued to dedicate long hours to arduous training. They worked hard when no one was looking, when the cameras were off. They wanted to become champions. Once they did, they wanted to win again and again, but why?

Federer has rewritten the record books, so what keeps him going? Fame? Ego? Money? Hardly. He simply loves the game, and he enjoys the physical and mental preparation prior to a tournament. He loves the challenge of competition, loves to be tested and pushed to his limits. [1] He loves developing his skills to new levels. The harder he works, the greater the satisfaction, and, yes, the more he wins. He has become a role model for us all. He is also a philanthropist and his foundation focuses on helping children living in poverty to take control of their future and actively shape it through early learning and education. [2] When his playing days are over, his legacy will live on. This is true for people in all fields of endeavor. Their love for what they do, that fervent passion, enables them to keep performing and advancing.

My esteemed mentor and friend, Russ Ackoff, wrote over thirty world-class books on leadership and management. His extraordinary accomplishments never gave him a sense of "arrival." In my last visit with him, two months before he passed away at age ninety, I was stunned by his enthusiasm and foresight. He said, "There is so much we can do.

With the people you know and the people I know, we can put something together to revolutionize education." He pulled out his pocket calendar and started to give me available dates for our next meeting. He did not look good physically, but it didn't matter. His desire, his vision for a better future, was enthralling.

Russ was undergoing hip surgery days after my visit. "Do you really need this surgery, Russ?" I asked.

"I hate to teach sitting down," he said.

Russ could have called it a day. He was already recognized as one of the most influential business thinkers of the twentieth century, but he had not "arrived" yet. His sense of purpose was stronger than his sense of accomplishment. He loved to teach and write, and he was planning to do more of both. His hip pain was in the way of enabling him to teach, and he could not teach under so much medication, so his decision to have surgery was driven by his passion to stay in the classroom. Unfortunately, his surgery led to complications that ultimately cost him his life.

From time to time, I would ask Russ for pointers on how to become a better teacher or how to become a published author. He used to say, "Teach because it is a good way to learn, and write because it's fun. Forget about publishing books. Write for yourself, enjoy the process, reflect on your own work, and share it with others if you want, but publishing is not as important as the act of writing."

These words removed the pressure I felt to write this book. I had become so consumed with publishing a book that I had missed the point of writing. The book was the destination, but I should have focused on the journey itself and enjoyed the process.

This book is now totally different from what I originally planned. I deviated from my original topic and even developed a different format. Some people will like it, and some will not. Some will criticize it and reject it, while others will embrace it. More importantly, I have experienced the wisdom of Russ's advice. It helped me crystallize my conviction that the notion of getting "there" is not as important as living in the here and now, having fun, experiencing how one's passion manifests itself, and committing anew to its pursuit.

If we commit to our vision now, we can look back in time and see that we are better off because of it. We can observe that we indeed made progress, made a difference, and along the way, made it possible for others to create their own futures. We can see that what we did has been of consequence and represents a meaningful legacy. These outcomes serve as powerful justifications for pursuing something that may have no end.

Maxim: When we try to shape our future, we shape ourselves in the process.

Chapter 15

Learning to Lead and Leading to Learn

We learn more by looking for the answer to a question and not finding it than we do from learning the answer itself.

—Lloyd Alexander, Fantasy Novelist

Learning begins with the question that we cannot answer!

Think for a moment about those who inspire you. Who are they, and why do they inspire you? How do they make you feel? What makes them unique? What are the intangibles that they possess? I am not talking about status. I'm asking you to reflect on the special characteristics or traits that set them apart. Make a list of those traits.

Now make a list of your own attributes, and then compare and contrast your own list of personal attributes with the attributes of those who inspire you. Look for similarities and differences, overlaps, and gaps.

Your lists will probably contain attributes such as the following:

- Self-control
- Cognitive fitness
- A contemplative mind
- Imagination and vision
- Innovation and creativity
- A disciplined will
- Perseverance
- Patience
- Self-confidence
- A strong, clear sense of purpose
- Integrity
- Curiosity
- Courage
- Intuition
- Passion
- Authenticity
- Wisdom
- Trustworthiness
- Caring
- Selflessness
- Charisma
- Inspiration

These attributes can be learned, but there are no academic courses to help you learn them. I've never met anyone who majored in curiosity or earned a degree in patience.

You can learn about these attributes through case studies and mentoring, but these approaches are predominantly descriptive and prescriptive methods of learning. Russ Ackoff observed, "Teaching, and therefore courses, cannot produce great leaders precisely because leadership is essentially an aesthetic activity. The most schools can do is provide some of the tools and techniques usable in creative work, but they cannot create creativity."[1] This does not mean that those tools and techniques cannot be taught to students as young as five years of age. In Stephen Covey's book *The Leader In Me*, he demonstrates how elementary school children are learning about how to get along with others, how to manage time wisely, how to take responsibility for themselves, and how to "to do the right thing even when no one is looking."[2]

While there is valuable information imparted through teaching, what we are taught is not as powerful as what we learn on our own. We can teach people to draw, but we cannot turn them into gifted artists.

This leads us to the perennial debate about whether leaders are born or developed. Some traits are innate, and others can be developed. The point is not to engage in a philosophical debate but to highlight the fact that we all have traits that, if acknowledged and harnessed, can be used to mobilize us in pursuit of a better future. It is about leveraging what we have and determining what we need to learn so that we can design and create the future we desire.

As I discussed earlier, to lead is to go first, to have the courage to articulate a desired new state, and to mobilize others and ourselves in its pursuit, regardless of the difficulty.

Leadership is not confined to organizational settings. On the contrary, leadership can be exercised anywhere, anytime. As we engage in the act of leading, we discover that learning begins with the questions we cannot answer, with scenarios that don't make sense, and with possibilities that are novel to us. We face tough choices. Through it all, we must be sensitive to the learning that emerges from these situations, open to these new life lessons.

The story that follows is a real-life example of how a team of students applied the CDDC cycle and how, by taking the lead and overcoming many obstacles, they made extraordinary contributions to the lives of children they didn't even know.

The story began in the spring of 2008 when Yana, one my students, watched an episode of the Oprah Winfrey show and was inspired by guest John Wood, the founder of a nonprofit organization called Room to Read. Wood was an up-and-coming Microsoft executive who quit his job to make a difference in the lives of the children of Nepal. He visited Nepal on vacation and was profoundly touched by the children he met.

Yana purchased a copy of Wood's book, *Leaving Microsoft to Change the World*.[3] After learning about the genesis of his foundation, she was intrigued about doing something similar in her native Ukraine, the largest country on the European continent. Ukraine became independent after the collapse of the Soviet Union in 1991. It had the lowest birth rate in Europe combined with the highest death rate. Poverty and poor health care were the two biggest problems facing Ukrainian children.

Such an endeavor could be overwhelming, particularly for a twenty-one-year-old student engaged in rigorous academic work, majoring in civil engineering, and looking for full-time employment. Yana had not led any major initiatives and had no significant professional experience to point to, but she had a big heart. She had a ton of passion but not much knowledge about how to get started.

Yana enrolled in my Systems Thinking course, where students propose a project idea to which they have a personal connection and where the outcome would have a positive consequence to society as a whole. After taking time to research various causes in Ukraine, she chose the idea of improving orphanage conditions. She read many articles about the deplorable conditions and lack of aid going to this cause. She knew that somebody should do something, and that somebody was her. Regrettably, she failed at first to create interest among the other students.

I thought that her topic deserved a second chance, but there was little we could do to make it part of the class. The students had already selected projects and formed teams according to the guidelines given to them, and Yana's project did not make the cut. I approached her to see if she would continue pursuing the idea outside of class. In a paper she wrote, she said, "To be honest, I had not considered embarking on this endeavor alone, but with Dr. Suárez's motivation and support, I knew

I could! I gifted Wood's book to Dr. Suárez, and over lunch, we began formulating ideas on how to put my vision into action." [4]

She presented me with a dedicated copy of the book, and while reading it, I became enthusiastic about the possibilities to advance her proposal. At the end of the semester, she told me that she would be visiting her family in Ukraine. I encouraged her to visit some orphanages so that she could connect with her proposal at a deeper level. She was already planning to do so. She was in the early stages of becoming a Leader of One.

She visited two orphanages in the Ternopil Region near her hometown. The first orphanage housed children under the age of three. The other, called Holy Family Orphanage, housed children of all ages up to eighteen. The chance to interact and play with the children touched her, and she was even more determined to find a way to help them. When she returned to the United States, we met again at the beginning of the semester. She had taken pictures of the children. I could sense her concern and her appreciation for the blessings she enjoyed in the United States since moving here in 1995.

I let her introduce the project as one of many proposed for the Quality Enhancement Systems and Teams (QUEST) capstone course, for which I served as faculty. She was thrilled, because this gave her a chance to keep her idea alive.

The day the project ideas were presented in class, she was nervous yet excited. We were not sure how the class would react to a project without a traditional "business" foundation but one based on philanthropy. We both took a gamble! The projects for this course were usually defined by corporations (clients) who then sponsored a team of students to work on their problem. Each student team served as a consultant group for the client. Throughout the semester, student teams met with the clients and faculty advisors to review possible solutions to problems under investigation. At the end of the semester, the students presented their findings at a public conference.

In Yana's case, there was no corporation backing the project, so there was no financial support—no client, no organizational champion or sponsor, not even an existing business process, no baseline, and no metrics of past performance. Her project was about shaping the future of the children in Ukraine. I knew that we would face pushback because it was not a traditional project and did not fit the existing paradigm, but I knew that we had to give it a chance. Even some of my colleagues and co-instructors challenged me. "How can you adopt a project without a sponsor or money? You are deviating from the guidelines. You are creating a dangerous precedent."

Yana was perceptive enough to know that her project was a departure from the norm and would face resistance from faculty, students, and guest panelists. Nevertheless, she made her presentation. It was her chance to lead and inspire, and she delivered! Not only did her classmates welcome the idea, but they flocked to her, asking to join her cause.

Yana had not taken any courses in business or engineering school on how to inspire others, yet she had succeeded. I could not have been more proud of her. It was the moment when the student becomes the teacher and, as teacher, I simply sat back and enjoyed the learning that was taking place.

The Shutters 4 Scholars (S4S) team was formed. It was a mix of business and engineering majors, each with a personal interest in helping the children. Each team member found his or her niche in the group. As the team leader and Ukrainian translator, Yana helped guide the team and maintained the relationship with the orphanages, and she worked out all of the logistics for the pilot program. Students Ellen and Allison developed a relationship with UCARE, Inc., a nonprofit organization with the goal of providing aid to Ukrainian orphans. Vladimir ("Vlad") is showcased in the next chapter, "From Idealization to Realization: The weBike Story," and Shaun, a computer major, designed and built the S4S website.

The word got out. Within days, Yana's project and its uniqueness was known even outside of class. Alexandra, a junior in the QUEST program and also from Ukraine, was drawn to the idea. She was not registered for the class, yet she asked me if she could be part of the team. (Another deviation from past practices, more resistance from my colleagues, and another gamble for me.) I supported her participation, and there she was, attending class, participating in team meetings, and making her contribution.

Alexandra said, "Joining this team simply felt right. I was born in Ukraine and have always had an interest in finding some way to give back to my roots. I am often moved by the opportunities I have in America, opportunities that most children, let alone orphans, do not have there."[5] It was remarkable to see her engagement and her commitment to this effort while managing her course work in finance and economics. Her academic load was demanding, yet she participated fully in team meetings and class sessions. She was always attentive in class, a witness to learning in action and its application to real life.

Alexandra was generous in her praise of this experience. "Through the course, a few ideas truly made an impact on me: the importance of having purpose, of pursuing your passions, idealizing your future, and working to get there. What struck me most, however, was Dr. Suárez's ability to empower the class, to inspire in people a sense of lifelong learning and improvement."[6]

Through this project, I learned more about the role that I have as an educator. It was not about teaching but inspiring people to learn. They did the work, asked the questions, explored the possibilities, developed the solutions, and worked around obstacles, financial constraints, language barriers, and differences in time zones. They succeeded not because I was teaching but because they were learning. They were inspired and willing to lead.

For Yana and Alexandra, this was a personal mission. It gave them a way to encourage these impressionable youth, who were living on the fringes of society, to escape the shocking statistics of their situation. In 2007, there were 112,000 Ukrainian orphans, or 1.11 percent of the total number of children in Ukraine (UNICEF).[7] Only 10 percent of these children were actually orphans. Ninety percent were "social orphans," subject to abuse from neglectful parents who then abandoned them. The children live in impoverished conditions, are often malnourished, and receive subpar education. They are typically forced to leave the orphanage system between the ages of fifteen and eighteen because of limited resources. Only about 27 percent of the orphans are able to find work. Sixty percent of girls end up in prostitution, and 70 percent of boys enter a life of crime (World Orphan Project).[8] About 10 percent have committed suicide by their eighteenth birthday.

As Russ Ackoff noted, inspiration without action is provocation. The team had gone through the first two of the four phases of the CDDC cycle: *Contemplation* and *Desire*. It was time to *Design* and *Create* something of value.

Their initial ideas included collecting money, clothing, and toys, and the improvement of the orphanage infrastructure. However, none of these ideas would represent enduring value for the orphans.

The team's interests were sparked anew when they began to discuss how much of their own future depended on the opportunity to attend college. Yana was reflective and appreciative of her opportunities. "Our education has shaped us in many positive ways.[9] We decided that our aim should be to help Ukrainian youth find access to higher education. This, in turn, can create more opportunity, such as allowing more orphans to attain better work."

The team was determined to accomplish their aim in a way that would engage the children. They discussed how a family in Africa successfully used photographs to bring attention to their plight for a better standard of living. They talked about the documentary *Born into Brothels*, where cameras changed the lives of a group of children in Calcutta, India.[10] The team was drawn to the idea that photography transcended language barriers and could show the children's stories in a compelling way, through their eyes. The team wanted to give the children a creative outlet and connect them to the world outside of the orphanage and to the financial aid that would support their higher education ambitions.

The S4S team began the Design stage and based the framework on four pillars: scholars, photography, technology, and sponsors. The children were the clients. They were defined by the S4S team as scholars of the world because they were internalizing and learning from their surroundings. The aim of the project was to increase opportunities for the orphans so that they could become successful adults. Photography would be the tool through which they would come to understand their society and their own lives. Cameras would encourage the children to express themselves and tell their stories, and they would allow them to build a vision of their futures. S4S would introduce the children to the world through the Internet.

Figure 7. Shutters 4 Scholars original website.

The development of the S4S website was critical to the project; it was a venue to share the photographs and biographies of the scholars. An online gallery would encourage interaction between the scholars and potential sponsors. Sponsors' donations would support a scholarship fund for the children.

The distillation of these ideas led to the articulation of a mission statement on the website. It reads, "Shutters 4 Scholars aims to empower young scholars to transform their own futures. Through the use of technology and photography, we break the geographic, economic, socio-cultural and language barriers that stand in the way of a brighter tomorrow. S4S recognizes that photography is a vehicle that can be used to engage youth in activities that improve their self-esteem and connect them to their community… The ultimate goal is to ensure they feel empowered to pursue their dreams and education and to give them the resources to do so." [11]

Effective Leaders of One focus on getting what they ideally want to create. The team members did exactly that. They wanted to connect with the Ukrainian youth in a positive way. By envisioning an ideal future for the children where they could grow and learn, the team was able to *shape* these outcomes, to commit them to a "blueprint." Their belief that change could occur as a result of this design strengthened their sense of purpose. They were able to create a call to action that would attract sponsors, and these sponsors would contribute the resources to make it happen.

Becoming legitimate in the eyes of the government was essential to attracting sponsors who would realize tax benefits from their donations. The team was not discouraged by the fact that they had to acquire governmental nonprofit status by the end of the semester. They partnered with an existing nonprofit organization, Ukrainian Children's Aid and Relief Effort (UCARE).[12] UCARE, Inc. had a scholarship program that provided living and educational support to orphans going to college or technical or trade school. UCARE was receptive to working with the team.

From this experience, the team learned that seemingly insurmountable obstacles can be overcome with creative thinking, that a "whole" can be created from disparate parts. The project taught them that there is a wealth of individuals and organizations with similar visions who are willing to share their knowledge and experience. This flow of information and ideas can help strengthen the effectiveness of any organization's cause. This partnership would also ensure that the project would be sustained even when the semester was over.

The S4S team used Yana's connection with the Holy Family Orphanage to launch the pilot program. The director of the orphanage was thrilled to have her students participate in the pilot program.

I purchased the disposable cameras for the team and arranged for them to be mailed to the children. Using disposable cameras dissolved technological obstacles such as differences in camera quality and computer access (to upload the photographs). The team decided to double the number of cameras that the scholars would need in case of malfunctions. They packed thirty disposable cameras and instructional pamphlets on camera operation, written in Ukrainian. Once the package arrived in Ukraine, Yana's cousin delivered it to the orphanage.

Nine students, ages ten to thirteen, volunteered to be photographers. The director told us that the children embraced the concept with great excitement and were able to follow through, capturing images that reflected aspects of their life.

Meanwhile, the team built the Shutters 4 Scholars website. It provided a link to the UCARE website and gave viewers an option to make donations to the scholarship fund through PayPal. After receiving the photographs and the children's biographies, the team posted them to the online gallery.

The semester's projects were presented at the QUEST Innovation and Consulting Conference, and the S4S team earned the award for Project of the Year. [13] Following the conference, S4S was featured in several publications[14] and on the weekly *Your Business and Money* program on Maryland Public Television. [15] The team received several monetary donations for the UCARE's scholarship program, demonstrating another maxim of this book: When you do the right thing and follow your passion, success follows you!

The hard work involved never seemed tedious. Ellen, one of the team members, put it best: "Everything that you do (in business school), you're always thinking about the bottom line and trying to make a profit. It's really nice to steer away from that and do something for the greater good and not necessarily in order to make the most money. We had not decreased cycle time or helped a client increase profits. Instead, we provided nine children, the ultimate clients, with an outlet for creative expression and hopefully a new outlook. Knowing that UCARE is still interested in continuing the partnership with S4S gave us a great sense of accomplishment."

UCARE is now interested in engaging its current college scholarship students in the photography program. The focus will be on technology in order to build computer skills and a better connection with the donors. The students will serve as role models to the younger orphans, so that they are encouraged to continue their education.

To make photography an educational experience, Shutters 4 Scholars is contemplating developing instructional aides to teach children in Ukraine the art of photography and how to use it as an educational tool to understand their society. The children's photographs can be exhibited in the United States to bring attention to their situation and made available for purchase. The funds will go toward their education.

As the team members moved into full-time careers after graduation, they carried with them a new sense of responsibility and connection with a world many miles away. As Yana and Alexandra put it, "We must allow children to see themselves differently. They must see their world in a new light; they must feel that they have a future after graduating from the orphanage system. That feeling must be made a reality. We hope that our efforts will help some of these young children overcome the brutality of their situation, that it will allow them to continue learning and to grow strong. It is up to us to help these children and young adults forge a meaningful future."

Sustaining Shutters 4 Scholars has been challenging for the team members as their careers began to take off and other life engagements became central to them. Notwithstanding these challenges, the fire still burns. Yana has stayed in contact with UCARE and has provided assistance with marketing and fundraising. The goal is to reinvigorate the program with UCARE by establishing a partnership with a camera distributor or sponsor to fund the cost of the digital cameras. The focus will be to make the photography an educational experience, using it to understand the society of the children and make better connections with their donors. The plans to engage current college UCARE scholarship students to participate in the photography program will be challenging given the political situation in Ukraine but the cause is worth pursuing. Stay tuned!

The S4S team offered a powerful example of leading to learn and learning to lead. Its efforts reflected how the experiential process can be intrinsic and enduring. Just as the S4S team did, experiential learning and the application of the Contemplation, Desire, Design and Creation cycle is enriched if we try new things, forgive our mistakes, welcome new perspectives, stay curious, and, above all, remain energized by our passion and desires.

The S4S team members built upon their individual strengths and talents. All of them, however, shared certain traits: a deep sense of caring, selflessness, passion, and authenticity. They recognized what they lacked and found ways to succeed in spite of any shortcomings.

This example illustrates how our learning and actions have an impact far beyond us when focused on a meaningful aim. It is unconscionable to pursue success if it benefits only us. Our actions always have a ripple effect on others. When we put others first, we create a lasting benefit and generate loyalty and trust with those we serve.

Reflection is crucial throughout the process, not just in the beginning. We need reflection to identify those interesting gaps between expectations, intentions, and results. Once we become aware of the gaps, we can seek a better way to address the dilemmas.

It's hard work, but it is our duty to ourselves and others to connect with our purpose, to nurture our passions, to seek out feedback, and to extract lessons from our actions. S4S proved that the things that matter most cannot be taught, but we can develop ways to learn them.

True learning takes place only when we have a deep sense of awareness, when we recognize our ignorance, and mitigate it by tapping into our strengths and leveraging our attributes. We learn by questioning commonly held assumptions and by being empathic, seeing life from the perspective of those we want to serve.

Maxim: The most meaningful lessons are seldom taught by others, but must be learned by you. It is through the act of interacting with the future that you want to create that you acquire meaningful learning and influence the future.

Chapter 16

From Idealization to Realization: The weBike Story

Good thoughts are no better than good dreams unless they be executed!

—Ralph Waldo Emerson, American Essayist and Poet

To choose to dream without taking action is, at best, entertainment, a fantasy, but fantasies have no basis in reality. Why dream and do nothing about it? Why tease ourselves with false hope?

Taking an idea and making it a reality requires both dream and design. Dreaming enables us to explore possibilities. As Victor Hugo noted, "There is nothing like a dream to create the future." [1] Dream and design together allow us to create vivid images that propel us toward a desired outcome.

Vlad came to see me after spending his summer in Germany. He was entering his senior year as a computer science major and a member of the QUEST multidisciplinary honors program. The summer overseas proved to be his time of contemplation. He was able to decompress from what had been a demanding academic year.

He had a vision about bringing a transportation sharing system to campuses and eventually to corporate settings and communities. What an audacious vision for a twenty-year-old Bulgarian with no history of entrepreneurship, no experience, no connections, and no financial backing. Moreover, he was aware that a similar system had been introduced in Washington, DC, and at the time it was floundering.

At the end of our meeting, we agreed that he would present his proposal before my Systems Thinking and Design class. We would put it through the CDDC cycle. The challenge was to translate his passion into the realm of possibility and move the concept from idealization to realization.

Vlad made a compelling case in class for the need and benefits of such a system. His drive and passion became contagious. He formed a team to design a transportation system that would enhance mobility on campus in the most effective and efficient way for all stakeholders.

Team members voiced their solid support. Members included Brad, a mechanical engineering major, Allie, a marketing major, and Yasha and Vlad, both computer science majors. Although the team connected to the concept emotionally and intellectually, each person had a unique perspective. Brad was most passionate about designing state-of-the-art bike stations. Allie was passionate about building a sense of community among the users. The bike system would be a means to that end.

Although each member had a different focus, the team shared a common aim of providing an eco-friendly, healthful, fun, and affordable transportation system on college campuses and in communities at large.

They began by assessing how a population of almost forty thousand students, staff, and faculty at the University of Maryland in College Park would benefit from a faster method of getting around campus. Their initial findings showed that 60 percent of the students who lived off campus, within a mile or two, drove cars, while a mere 8 percent of students used a bicycle. The current university transportation system in College Park was neglecting the needs of the community. Parking was expensive and hard to find. Public transportation was unreliable. Traffic congestion was damaging the environment. The status quo would lead to continued environmental damage as well as the continuance of a broken public transportation system. What an opportunity for the university to embrace such a system and showcase its role as a national leader with an environmentally sound campus transportation system.

As the semester drew to a close, this rudimentary vision progressed through the CDDC cycle from contemplation to creation. The buy-in from the team members grew stronger as they discussed their personal commitment to doing well by doing good and giving back to society. The next stage was to engage in the design of the system. They saw themselves not in the "biking business" but in community building, and to capture this perspective, they coined the name, *weBike*.

During the design phase, the team adopted the idealized design methodology and brainstormed the positive and negative implications associated with introducing their concept on campus. The idealized design addressed six components: bicycles, stations, website, community, users, and environment.

Here are samples of the design specifications for each component.

- **Bikes**

  - Durable and well maintained

  - Adjustable for different-sized users

  - Intuitive for beginners to ride

  - Available storage space for backpacks, laptops, etc.

- **Stations**

  - To be placed in high-traffic locations

  - To be accessible via student ID

  - To be stocked continuously with bikes

  - To be powered by eco-friendly technology (i.e., solar)

- **Website**

  - Would allow users to monitor bike locations and check bike racks

  - Would provide user profiles to track mileage biked and calories burned

- **Community**

  – Connect users to one another to encourage shared values

  – Foster passion for biking through events, rides, and classes

  – Promote a sustainable lifestyle

  – Seek development of bike legislation and bike-friendly community paths

The team envisioned the following benefits:

- **Users**

  – Fastest form of campus transportation; saves time in between classes

  – Ease of use, simplicity of bikes with automatic shifters

  – Safety features such as brightly colored bikes with lights installed for night riding

  – User-friendly payment process using portable devices and technology

  – Flexibility in route choice and destination

  – Responsibilities of bike ownership and maintenance eliminated

  – Sense of community instilled

- **Environment**

  – University of Maryland recognized as a leader in green transportation on campus

  – Traffic congestion decreased; need for new parking spaces on campus reduced

  – CO_2 emissions reduced

- Cost of purchasing new vehicles for official campus use and building new parking garages eliminated

- Prospective students and eco-minded faculty drawn to the school

The team applied interactive planning to work backward from the idealized design. When you use this approach, you use the future to plan for the present, initiating steps to close the gap between an ideal design and the current reality. As part of these efforts, the team recognized that the introduction and success of their idea would not be possible without influencing the attitudes of all of the stakeholders, receiving support from the university leadership and the State of Maryland Department of Transportation, and establishing strategic relationships with sponsors and suppliers.

The team surveyed the market by gathering prospective user feedback and their attitudes toward the concept. They garnered press and media attention, presented the concept at campus-wide exhibits, and formed relationships with university and state officials. At the same time, they met with intellectual property lawyers to protect their idea and business model.

After these sessions, they refined the concept of how the system and the customer would interface, creating a system that could function effectively with little or no staff. [2]

Joining the weBike community would be easy. Prospective users would enter their contact information into the weBike website and in so doing agree to the terms, conditions, and rules of engagement for riders. The users' personal information and cellphone numbers would be archived in the database. Once this was done, they could access the bikes. Each bike would be clearly identified with an ID number.

Figure 8. weBike's original website.

The weBike system would use a text-message platform and web-based application to link users to the server. When users wanted to check out a bike, they sent a text message to weBike with the ID number of the bike they wanted to use. The system authenticated the text message to ensure that the request came from a registered user. Within seconds, the system sent a reply to the user with the code needed to unlock the bike. Once the rider arrived at his or her destination, the rider was responsible for locking the bike and texting weBike to inform the system of arrival at the destination. The bike was ready for use by the next customer.[3]

Once the team had a design and concept of operation for the bike-sharing system, they conducted an exercise to assess the implications of introducing the system. The idea was to uncover any relevant and consequential implications from introducing a community bike system on campus.

This exercise proved invaluable in uncovering negative implications related to accidents, lawsuits, theft, and other adverse possibilities as well as positive ones. The design was vetted and tested. The integration of these methods—idealized design, interactive planning, and the exploration of positive and negative implications—allowed the team to develop a comprehensive blueprint of its vision and a solid framework for action.

The team suffered setbacks. University leaders could not be persuaded to adopt a campus-wide initiative even though it was the ideal setting, given the high concentration of young people who needed to move from building to building in a speedy and cost-effective manner. The team hit a "bureaucratic wall of resistance." The second setback was the realization that the bike station component was not feasible economically, and it proved to be technologically challenging.

The team came to see me for advice. After describing the challenges with the station, my advice came in the form of a question. I asked how they could implement weBike *without* stations: "What if you don't have station at all?" They seemed dumbfounded, and after a few second, new possibilities emerged, and the system was brought back to life, hope restored. The team turned a negative into a positive. A station-less system design became a point of pride for the team and a feature of competitive advantage, because they now had no need for large upfront expenses.

They faced adversity in their journey to shape the future. Skeptics tried to persuade them to abandon the project or copy existing bike-sharing business models. Time after time, their relentless passion prevailed. As team member Allie noted, "You can't expect everyone to share your passion, so you have to develop a way for them to see it through your eyes. You have to be both energetic and patient in order to stick with your idea. You have to create your own momentum."

The team continued working on other aspects of the design, and they continued translating challenges into opportunities and barriers into bridges. They focused on developing relationships with city and county government officials, seeking ways by which the concept could gain traction. They approached student organizations, seeking funding and investment. They established partnerships with a bike supplier and local bike establishments in College Park. Everything they did mattered, and in time, it all came together.

Along the way, the team experienced fear, frustration, doubt, rejection, and disappointment. They learned firsthand that things may not go according to plan, and they learned how crucial it was to continually adapt to changing circumstances and to overcome obstacles by examining a negative as if it were a positive. As the team proudly said, "One must learn how to compensate for lack of resources with resourcefulness."

They were confronted with the harsh reality that they had no money, no support from politicians and leaders, and they were facing an army of doubters. They also learned that the fear of failure can be overcome by visioning and passion. Allie put it this way: "Visioning allows you to build something with resources that don't yet exist. It lets you develop a platform that you can grow from. Once you have the vision, you can develop new ideas and plans and take action. Without visioning, as a team of college kids with no experience and no financial capital, we would never have been able to create a system of bike sharing to get to and from campus."

weBike became a reality at the Mazza GrandMarc Apartments (a $43 million complex, the first student housing in North College Park, Maryland, with over six hundred beds). The complex targeted graduate students. Its population and proximity to campus made it a great setting to build the weBike community of riders. A North College Park website that focused on environmental issues pointed out in an article that weBike represented the country's first station-less model of bike sharing. The reporter interviewed users, and one rider remarked that he used the bikes almost every day of the week. weBike was his primary form of transportation, and he much preferred it to waiting for a bus. The Mazza GrandMarc management offered the system to its residents free of charge. Ridership was increasing steadily, and text-message feedback from users was all positive. The station-less model was far less expensive than other systems such as one in Washington, DC, where each station required about $35,000 to build.

The Mazza GrandMarc offered a model for future subscribers. Future clients—municipalities, the university, a community developer, or a corporate campus director—will pay monthly for the service. They will pay upfront for the equipment (bikes, locks, and web server) as well as a monthly fee to have weBike manage the system operations. Contracts between weBike and clients will make it clear that weBike does not own the equipment and is not responsible for its care. weBike envisions that the client will hire and pay for someone to maintain its fleet. This supports the concept that as multiple systems begin to operate at one time, each will be basically self-sufficient.

The team has been showcased on Think MTV, profiled twice on the cover page of the *Diamondback*, the official University of Maryland Campus newspaper, [4] in "The City Fix." [5] The team won the Green Maryland Project of the Year award and presented the concept at the QUEST Innovation and Consulting Conference. It also received donations from individuals and small businesses.

As the concept gains momentum, the weBike community may influence the users in other aspects of their lives. weBike is not just about biking. It's about changing the way people move about so that they coexist in harmony with the environment.

The team has provided people with a choice of travel. They are now transitioning weBike to an open-sourced bike-share project that enables any campus or small community to model the technology and create its own station-less bike-share system. These actions are contributing to a better future for all. The weBike team members pulled the future into the present.

Only when we are courageous enough to admit that we don't know something do we give learning a chance. Shaping the future will expose you to failure and force you to meet ignorance along the way. There are no experts when we are dealing with a new reality. At moments, you will be confronted with the fact that you do not know what to do, and those around you may not know either. You will make mistakes, and the devastating forces of failure and doubt may surprise you. Remain anchored in your passion, your values, and your aim.

The members of weBike are proving how following one's passion can make a meaningful difference in the world. As I learned from the weBike team, a key to success is to "embrace the challenges associated with your passion, because they will lead you to discovery and invention."

Maxim: A dream without action is a fantasy. Action without purpose is a random act. Dreams designed and fueled by passion have the power to transform the present and shape the future.

Chapter 17

A Leadership Imperative: Finding Your Ethical North

> *Assume responsibility for outcomes as well as for the processes and people you work with. How you achieve results will shape the kind of person you become.*

—C. K. Prahalad, Corporate Strategist and Distinguished University Professor, University of Michigan

After reading the stories of Shutters 4 Scholars and weBike, you may wonder if the accomplishments of these young leaders were due only to the fact that their efforts were started from scratch. They did have the advantage of not having to "destroy" an existing organization. In this sense, they had a leg up in the process, but this approach can be effective in existing organizations. The White House Communications Agency example demonstrated that even when there is a culture of tradition, protocol, stiff policies and regulations, and high-stakes politics, the transformative CDDC cycle is equally powerful.

Will these concepts work in a corporate setting where internal competition, external competitiveness, shareholder pressures, envy, egos, and money are involved? Yes, they will, and they must!

Corporations of any size offer a great setting for applying these concepts. Just as we have individual purposes and aspirations, businesses have meaningful purposes and collective aspirations. This cycle is rooted in principles, and their application will bring value to individuals, teams, and organizations of all kinds. I consider it a leadership and a moral imperative to align and mobilize resources in an organization to enable its people to achieve their potential while the organization optimizes its resources and accelerates its competitive advantage. Leaders must embrace the notion that enduring success can come only from the human spirit.

In an insightful keynote address in Washington, DC, Bob Stevens noted, "All businesses are people businesses...It is the role of leadership to help others achieve their professional aspirations." [1] These simple yet profound statements underscore the importance of seeking alignment between individual and collective aspirations and between personal and organizational goals. When passions are aligned to a common purpose, people do great things, and organizations enhance their performance and expand their positive impact to stakeholders and society as a whole.

Stevens was sharing a deeply felt personal conviction that taking care of people and helping them do well is a leadership imperative and a prerequisite for the organization to do well.

Leadership is required to create a culture of authentic engagement. Such a culture is challenging to create, because dynamics in the workplace can be treacherous. The organizational setting offers many opportunities but also a hypercomplex social context within which the pursuit of your desired future can steer you into a minefield. It is an arena prone to developing winners and losers and where a "winner take all" culture permeates. The need for instant gratification, incentives, bonuses, and promotions may lead people to take "integrity shortcuts" to advance their personal agendas and prevent others from advancing. They may succeed in the short term, but the damage to their colleagues and the organization will be long lasting.

Aligning individual success and collective success is never easy. Even when you try your best to do the right things for the right reasons, perceptions and distortion of your motives may trigger unwanted reactions. As Stephen Covey noted, "We judge ourselves by our intentions and others by their actions."[2]

Your success may represent a threat to those around you. Even a superior may feel insecure having competent, assertive, visionary subordinates. Your sense of direction and clarity of conviction in pursuit of your dream may become a source of resentment and envy. Often, those who don't know what they want, or who don't know how to properly get what they want, may want what you have. They benchmark their desires against those of others and look everywhere but within to find out what they want. They may apply tactics of resistance and retaliation to sabotage you. They may withdraw support at critical moments and exploit your talents for their personal gain. "Friendly fire" is not uncommon.

Because shaping your future and that of your organization can be under siege, authentic leadership becomes critical. The leadership that I'm talking about is not simply driven by rank or position. The position is important, but strong principles and values are essential if leaders are to use their power and knowledge effectively. Such leaders have the resiliency and desire to do the right thing for all their people. As Stevens suggests, it is of vital importance not just to do well but to do good along the way.

At one point in my career, I was charged with radically transforming a critical component of an organization. Tough decisions had to be made in order to bring the entity to peak performance. I was enticed by the challenge and committed to turning the operation around. It was too important and too vital to be ignored, so I embraced it with a high sense of duty, hope, and optimism.

I had done similar work in perhaps the toughest setting in the world, the White House, and I knew that such transformations are tough and require patience and sharing the vision and the process with those who will be affected by it.[3] Transformations also require support from the leader. This endorsement cannot simply be a "go ahead, and I'll support you," but more of a "we are all in this together" kind of backing.

My boss publicly stated that I had the toughest job in the organization: leading change. An alarm went off the day he said, "You have a lot of goodwill capital in this institution. Use it." He viewed my goodwill as a tool to accelerate the agenda, but to me, goodwill was not a possession, not like money in the bank that I could spend to buy what I wanted or save for eventualities.

To me, goodwill is an integral part of *who* I am. Goodwill cannot be used as a means to manipulate others. If we do so, it is no longer goodwill. As leaders, we must stay true to our core values. No organizational goal is worth giving away who we are.

Stevens' words resonated with me and guided me to avoid the temptation of taking ethical shortcuts. I did my best to follow his advice to do well but do good along the way.

Enduring success requires a genuine desire to bring about change without compromising our personal tenets, being guided by our "ethical north." We cannot compartmentalize who we are separate from what we are asked to do. Our actions must balance the dignity of the individuals involved with the well-being of the organization. This balance is not always possible, but pursuing it with authenticity sends a strong message to others and helps strengthen our moral backbone.

In this book, I emphasize the importance of connecting with your core values and the notion of honoring who you are. I believe that it is precisely in tough times—when expectations are high, options are tough—that we must rely on our beliefs to ensure that we do the right things right. The harsh realities of the workplace and the pressures to meet imposed expectations will test you repeatedly and might push you to the brink of moral bankruptcy.

In tough situations, your strength will not come from money, title, power, or influence but from your capacity to leverage intangibles: the things that can't be hoarded yet good people have in abundance, the things that we can't buy yet we own, and the things that we will have forever because we have given them to others. These intangibles make up your moral compass, your ethical north. In times of turbulence, when fear pervades an organization, they will guide you.

We can't confuse what we do with who we are. Titles and jobs do not define us. What we do is constantly subject to the manipulation of colleagues and superiors by means of bonuses, promotions, power, the pursuit of prestige, and the perennial "carrots and sticks." Who we are transcends labels no matter how important a position is.

In 1962, when John F. Kennedy was pursuing a bid for the presidency, he was confronted with the conflict between who he was and what he did. The issue of religion was delicate for him and given what was at stake, Kennedy chose to say, "I am not the Catholic candidate for president. I am the Democratic candidate who happens to be a Catholic." [4] To this day, the quote generates controversial debate, because it underscores the struggle between core values and external roles.

The tension generated by the tug of war between who we are and what we do will always be with us. The stakes may not be as high as those of Kennedy, when national interests were at play, but in the chambers of our soul, the stakes will always be high. When we abandon who we are because of ambition, ego, prestige, power, control, or influence over others, we put the essence of our lives at stake.

A colleague of mine was persuaded to take a temporary assignment as the interim director of a critical function within an organization. She had recently joined the institution and found herself unexpectedly leading the team. It was not the position for which she had been hired. She expressed her reluctance to take this assignment, but the pressure to do so was high, and she felt that she had no choice. She wanted to make a good impression and be perceived as a team player, so she "took one for the team." She explained how she had cautiously accepted what apparently she did not want. "I have no options," she said. She was offered higher temporary pay, a leadership title, and the promise of brighter days ahead.

In an earlier chapter, I asked if you were an artist or a critic. Are you in control of your life, or is someone else "painting your canvas"? I believe that my colleague had relinquished control and that her "canvas" was being painted for her. She opted for promises of a higher salary and increased status. You can't go wrong with that, right?

Three months later, she found herself experiencing resistance and resentment from the team. The pressures from above were intense. She was trapped in the middle of a toxic dynamic, and she came to my office to vent. "I feel that my life is out of control, and there is nothing that I can do about it at this point." Notice how she did not say that her *work* was out of control or that her working relationships or capacity to lead were out of control. Her whole life was out of control! The things that were appealing at the time—the money, promotions, and the things that would supposedly bring her a brighter future—were impacting the only thing that mattered: her life! Accepting such an appointment was leading to helplessness, resentment, and burnout. Unfortunately, too many of us feel our lives are out of control because of what we accept as the cost of making a living.

Although I sympathized with her, I believed that her life was out of control by choice. She knew that something was wrong but didn't take action to correct it. Letting go or putting up with something is a matter of choice.

Think of the accidents caused by drunk drivers. They happen because in most cases the drivers are convinced that they are fine. They think, "I can drive, I can handle it." These are their typical responses when someone tries to take away their keys, but they don't surrender the keys because they are not aware of how ominous their situation is. Their judgment is impaired, and their capacity to see the implications of their actions is blurred.

When we say, "My life is out of control," it is up to us to "give up the keys" and "get out from behind the steering wheel." Ignoring the warning signs is a conscious choice. What prevents you from taking the right action? A bad economy? A poor performance appraisal? Fear of repercussions? Not being considered for a promotion? My colleague put up with a temporary appointment that generated permanent disappointment. She eventually asked to be transferred to another department, but things were never the same. The experience left profound fault lines in her foundation and she eventually quit.

If you are defined by what you do, the most superficial aspects of work (promotions, bonuses, and so on) become the ends. If that is what you choose, you must accept the consequences of your choice. You are choosing to have others control you, to have others "paint your canvas."

It takes courage to change, but it will not be possible if you have forgotten who you are. Where you are going cannot be separated from how you get there. The "why" and the "how" are as important as the "what" and the "where."

In one of my executive MBA sessions, I asked the group to reflect on the characteristics that they admired about leaders who had influenced them the most, the people who had been an example for them, those that they would be willing to work for anytime. I gave them one minute to think about those attributes and then asked for volunteers to share their reflections with the group.

"Caring," said the first one. "Genuine," shouted another. The participation gained momentum. "Authentic." "Resilient." "Puts others first." "Visionary." "Inspiring." "Trustworthy." "Transparent."

I started to write the attributes on the board, but I could not keep up. Not one person, not even the senior executives, used words such as "power," "manipulative skills," "capacity to broker deals behind the scenes," "ability to control others," or "smarter than anyone in the room."

These latter descriptors reflect leaders with shallow foundations— people who protect their jobs above all else, who stand behind a title to hold onto power, or who move up without going deep.

The difference between a leader and someone who is merely in a leadership position is stark. Good leaders believe in the capacity of their people. They understand that the job of a leader is always bigger than one person. They trust their people and enable them. They make those around them better performers. They know when to delegate and when to take over. They are present in good times but connected in tough ones. In the darkest moments, they say, "Follow me!"

I saw this firsthand at the White House. My concept of leadership was shaped by seeing world leaders in action, addressing momentous events that required a balance between strength and compassion, decisiveness and flexibility, principle and practicality, speed and prudence, and responsibility and accountability. Most importantly, they required a willingness to accept, own, and learn from the unintended consequences of decisions.

Anyone can lead in good times, but true leaders have the patience, resilience, clarity, and audacity to lead when things are messy. They put collective interest over self-interest and always put their people first. They understand that it cannot be about them but about the cause that they represent. They know that they are not just leading a business; they are advancing a purpose. As I learned during my years in the White House Military Office, "People first, mission always!"[5]

There are those in leadership positions who move up but do not possess the most desirable leadership attributes. They are typically impatient, pressuring others for faster results. They lack an appreciation that transformation cannot be rushed. You cannot plant a seed and rush the process of growth. Fertilizer and water must be added in judicious amounts. If you exceed those limits, people become psychologically "saturated" and overwhelmed by demands.

Recognition in good times is always welcome, but ownership and support in tough times are a must. Those who are merely occupying a leadership position but lack authentic leadership attributes tend to be supportive when things are going well. In fair winds and following seas, they make you feel like part of the crew. But when the boat is leaking, when the storm is approaching, and the surf is rough, they quickly jump into the emergency raft.

Think of Captain Chesley "Sully" Sullenberger's dramatic crash landing of the US Airways Flight 1549 in the Hudson River in New York on January 15, 2009. His copilot was flying that mission, but when the engines died, he took over by putting his hand on the side stick, an aviation protocol to transfer control. "My aircraft," he said to the copilot. [6] It became his plane, and it was time to lead in difficult times. As he was exploring the options at hand, he did not blame the copilot for not avoiding the birds that hit the engines. He did not jump off in a parachute to save his life. He did not say, "This is your mess." He owned it and took charge, and through his actions, he conveyed to the crew and all the passengers, "We will be fine, follow me!"

He was the first to take ownership of the situation and the last one to exit the plane. Through his actions, all 155 passengers and crew members came out of the crash unscathed. This miracle on the Hudson River exemplifies leadership at its best.

Captain Sullenberger rocketed to fame, and in every event, he was quick to diffuse the attention given to him. He profusely and consistently praised his crew who helped ditch the plane safely, saying, "It was a crew effort." [7] He made all the right moves, and he was recognized as a hero, a pilot's pilot, the consummate pilot. Through his grace, dignity, deep values, competence and concern for others, he demonstrated to the world that how we act is who we are. His actions gave every passenger and crew member on board a second chance.

Shaping the future is your choice. You can do it or not, but to do so takes leadership guided by your ethical north, a visceral sense of a desire for a better future, and the courage and commitment to do the right things right.

Maxim: Where you are going cannot be separated from how you are getting there.

Chapter **18**

Trust Is the Glue

Trust is the highest form of human motivation. It brings out the very best in people, but it takes time and patience.

—Stephen Covey, Self-Help Advocate, Author, Lecturer

In 1994, a friend and colleague invited me to a Washington, DC, Chamber of Commerce session to serve as part of the audience for a North American telecast of Dr. Stephen Covey, world-renowned author, speaker, and consultant. He was promoting his latest book, *First Things First*, a self-help book intended to help people achieve effectiveness by organizing their lives around the priorities or "first things" that matter most.[1]

I was excited about this opportunity. In 1996, Covey was regarded by *Time* as one of the twenty five most influential Americans. His bestselling book, *The 7 Habits of Highly Effective People*, was named the most influential business book of the twentieth century.[2] I was a student of his work and was being trained at the Covey Leadership Center to serve as facilitator of The Seven Habits of Highly Effective People workshops.

I thoroughly enjoyed the presentation, which I considered insightful and pragmatic. It was a real treat to take a break from my hectic work at the White House and see Covey, whom I so much admired, in person. I felt invigorated by his lecture. At the end of the session, I thanked my colleague for the opportunity, and he asked me if I would like to meet Covey. "Sure," I replied. This was the icing on the cake! I couldn't go wrong with meeting Covey in person—at least that's what I thought.

I was taken to a small room where they were taking off his makeup and the wireless lapel microphone. As I was introduced, my friend added, "Gerald works across the street at the White House." Covey looked at me with a penetrating gaze and said, "Really?" I nodded. He said, "Did you know, Gerald, that I've always wanted to make a presentation to the president and the presidential staff? They would benefit so much from this material. It is a dream of mine to make such a presentation."

I thought but could not express out loud, *Thank you for sharing your dream, but it is not easy to influence the president's schedule.* I listened with diplomacy and exited gracefully. As I was leaving the room, with a thunderous voice, Covey yelled, "Gerald, I empower you to make it happen!" I waved goodbye and thought, *Oh boy!*

A few days later, I received a Federal Express package from Provo, Utah: a copy of *First Things First.* The book was inscribed with a personal note from Covey: "Make it happen, Gerald! Your friend, Stephen."

I felt a sense of duty to give it a shot. I stayed active facilitating in-house Seven Habits of Highly Effective People sessions, building a critical mass to gain support for a possible visit. I had several meetings with the leadership, but the idea did not gain traction because of operational priorities.

I kept trying, because I thought that bringing Covey to the White House would boost our efforts to enhance the organizational culture and create an atmosphere of synergy and trust that would help us perform better.

Several months went by. I had made no progress until I spotted my boss, the Honorable Joseph J. Simmons IV, carrying a stack of documents, including a copy of *The 7 Habits of Highly Effective People.*

A serendipitous gift! During our next stand-up meeting (a daily morning meeting at the White House to go over the schedule and movements of the principals), my boss lifted up his copy of the book and said,

"Everyone in this room should read this book. It is a very good book, but most importantly, the president is reading it, and at least we need to be buzzword compliant."

I seized the moment, raised my hand, and suggested that we could bring the author in for a session in the West Wing. Because the president was reading the book, perhaps he would be interested in attending. Mr. Simmons was against it. It would cost too much. Capitalizing on the inscription in my book from Covey and trusting in the magic of empowerment, I said, "He is my friend, sir!" Simmons was adamant. He did not want to put the organization in the position of paying exorbitant fees for a high-profile consultant and, more importantly, did not want to accept a free presentation from a consultant. Either one would bring unwanted attention and might derail the benefit of having the session.

I said, "Sir, don't worry about that. Stephen and I are good friends."

With some reluctance, he said, "Well, Doc, tread lightly."

That was my cue to call Covey. I placed the call and was told that he was in a meeting, but after identifying my affiliation with the White House, Covey came on the line. After the amenities, I addressed his dream of making a presentation at the White House. He was thrilled, and we found a way to meet the requirements to make this possible.

Covey arrived in Washington the night before his session along with his assistant of many years, Ms. Nancy Aldridge. I greeted him at the hotel and gave him an overview of the schedule, which would include a VIP tour of the staterooms as well as of the East and West Wings. During the tour, Covey absorbed every detail and expressed an appreciation for the building and its history.

We scheduled a presentation for the White House Communications and the White House Military Office staffs, an evening session for the West Wing staff, and a breakfast meeting with President Clinton in the Oval Office.

I escorted Covey and Aldridge from the hotel to the southwest appointment gate of the White House where the Secret Service processed visitor badges. The Secret Service agents inside the armored booth opened a metal drawer and, using the speaker system, asked the two visitors for picture identifications. Aldridge pulled her driver's license from her purse and gave it to me, and I put it in the drawer. The process worked as expected. All the information from our guests had been given to the Secret Service ahead of time; the Secret Service had conducted the security protocols prior to their arrival.

It was now time to do the same for Dr. Covey. He had only to do the same as Ms. Aldridge, but he didn't. The Secret Service asked for picture identification. He pulled his wallet and gave me what appeared to be a driver's license, but it was a wallet-sized picture of his family. I looked at the picture and turned and looked at him, signaling that he had not given me a picture ID. He whispered, "Go ahead, give it to them...let's see what happens!"

"Stephen," I said, "we don't do things with the Secret Service just to see what happens."

"Trust me," he said, "it's going to be fun!" I didn't think so. He whispered, " I do this all the time. I just like to tease people."

He insisted, and I dropped the picture in the drawer. I took a few steps back and let him face the agents directly. They reacted as soon as they looked at the picture. "Sir, there's a mistake, this is not a picture... "

Covey said, "A mistake? That cannot be. Let me see."

The agent turned the picture back, and Covey told them that there was no mistake. "This, is, indeed, my family—my lovely wife and all our children."

The agent told him that they still needed a picture ID. As I anticipated, the Secret Service was not in a humorous mood, but Covey was not done. When asked for a government-issued ID, he asked why. This was 1994, when the world was quite different. The agent replied that he needed to verify who he was.

Covey said, "Oh, that's simple. I'm Stephen Covey! If you need further evidence, Nancy can verify this. She has been with me for over twenty-five years. Gerald can also validate this. He works here, and he is my friend."

Not so fast, I thought.

It was apparent that the agents would stick to the operating procedures. A Secret Service agent picked up the mic and said, "Sir, you have a beautiful family, loyal colleagues, and good friends, but if you want to come in and meet with the president, we need to see a picture ID. It is standard security protocol."

Covey turned toward me with a big grin and said, "I don't think that they trust me!" He proceeded to give the agents a driver's license, and while they were processing his badge, he said, "I gave them what matters most to me: my word, my family, and my friends. Anyone can fake an ID."

Covey's prank gave me a lesson about trust that still resonates in my mind. To him, trust is the glue of life! It is the element that lubricates human communication and sustains enduring relationships. There are different levels of trust. One is conscious trust. We trust consciously because we have seen evidence or have experienced something. This kind of trust is captured in President Ronald Reagan's signature phrase, "Trust but verify." The other kind is unconditional trust. There is no need to validate something because we believe it at a deeper, visceral level.

When the level of trust is high, people are open to express their thoughts, feelings, and opinions. They are open to share information, ideas, knowledge, and experiences. In the absence of trust, people tend to behave evasively, defensively, and even inconsiderately.

Trust is a delicate construct that takes many years to build and just one act to destroy. It is a necessary condition for cooperation and communication and an essential component in shaping our future.

As you pursue a better future, it is valuable to seek answers to questions that address your perspective on trust:

- Do you trust your intuition?

- Do you trust your level of knowledge?

- Do you trust your skills?

- Do you trust your vision of your future?

- Do you trust the people around you?

- Do you trust your capacity to adapt and deal with uncertainty?

A Leader of One answers these questions with a resounding yes, even in the absence of evidence.

Trust begets trust, an essential lubricant that nurtures positive thinking and interpersonal relationships, but in the absence of conscious trust, in the absence of quantifiable evidence, what should we do? The way ahead becomes torturous when the trade-offs are confusing, the data inconclusive, and the outcomes uncertain. The sentiments of doubt and perceived risk can combine to become a psychological time bomb.

When embarking on a new and challenging endeavor, it tends to seem scarier that it actually is. Nelson Mandela noted, "It always seems impossible until it's done."

In 1492, Christopher Columbus did not have all the data he needed to succeed. In fact, he severely underestimated the circumference of the earth. We can arguably say that when he left on his journey, he did not know with precision where he was going. When he arrived, he did not know exactly where he was. When he returned, he was confused about where he had been. The details of his trip were wrong, but the overall accomplishment was a breakthrough of the times. He had seen a new world. [3]

Columbus opened up new possibilities and, through his trips, initiated and sustained contact between Europeans and indigenous Americans. Columbus took risks and trusted his navigational skills. He seemed to have an unquestionable belief that he could adapt to the conditions he would face along the way. He faced rough winds, ferocious seas, drifting currents, and an embattled and skeptical sailing crew, but he persevered until he found new land. He was able to refine his maps and embark on even more courageous voyages.

Like Columbus, we face adversity as we chart a new future. Our skills will be tested, our knowledge questioned, and our motives scrutinized. Just as Columbus did, we must embrace the challenge with trust, courage, and the conviction that there is a future worth the sacrifice.

The rewards of being a Leader of One are many, but the process of becoming one will not be easy. We will have tough choices to make but must pursue our aim with trust and resolve. As Theodore Roosevelt said, "In any moment of decision, the best thing you can do is the right thing. The next best thing is the wrong thing, and the worst thing you can do is nothing." [4]

I hope that you adopt the Contemplation, Desire, Design, and Creation cycle to discover the right thing for you. Find your purpose, trust your vision, and become a Leader of One. For if you do, your future will mostly be influenced by you, not by *them, they* or *it*. Never be afraid of failure, but always be afraid of not trying.

Go forth and prosper. It's your future. Shape it!

Compilation of Creation Phase Questions

- Wouldn't it be nice if...

- What if I (we) tried...

- What is keeping me (us) from doing...

- Is there a difference between my (our) intentions and my (our) results?

- How do others perceive the results? How do I (we) know?

- Do I (we) make choices based on expectations of others?

- What point of view or role most influences my (our) actions (e.g., parent, friend, colleague, boss)?

- Do I (we) play it safe because of fear of failure?

- How much do habits and tradition guide my (our) choices?

- What are my (our) initial assumptions? Are they validated or denied throughout the creation process?

- In what other ways could I (we) have thought about this action that I (we) did not at the time?

- How would my future look like if I had no excuses?

- How would my life look like if I could not blame anyone for my past?

- Am I "owning" the results? Am I taking responsibility for the consequences of my actions?

- Am I extending my present out into the future or pulling the desired future into the present?

- Do I trust my intuition?

- Do I trust my level of knowledge?

- Do I trust my skills?

- Do I trust my vision of my future?

- Do I trust the people around me?

- Do I trust my capacity to adapt and deal with uncertainty?

Notes

Preface

1. Stephen Covey, *The 7 Habits of Highly Effective People: Powerful Lessons in Personal Change* (New York: Fireside, 1989).
2. T.S. Eliot, *The Complete Poems and Plays: 1909-1950* (Boston: Houghton Mifflin Harcourt, 1952).
3. R. L. Ackoff, J. Magidson, and H. Addison, *Idealized Design: How to Dissolve Tomorrow's Crisis...Today* (Upper Saddle River, NJ: Wharton Publishing, 2006).
4. Gandhi, http://thinkexist.com/quotation/one_man_cannot_do_right_in_one_department_of_life/340611.html.
5. http://www.morehouse.edu/about/chapel/mays_wisdom.html.

Introduction

1. R. L. Ackoff, "A Brief Guide to Interactive Planning and Idealized Design," http://www.ida.liu.se/~steho/und/htdd01/AckoffGuidetoIdealizedRedesign.pdf.
2. *Merriam-Webster's Collegiate Dictionary*, 10th ed. (Springfield, MA: Merriam-Webster, Inc., 1998).
3. John Donne, http://www.luminarium.org/sevenlit/donne/meditation17.php.
4. J. Dominguez and V. Robin, *Your Money or Your Life: Transforming Your Relationship with Money and Achieving Financial Independence* (New York: Penguin, 1992).
5. C. Handy, *The Elephant and the Flea: Reflections of a Reluctant Capitalist* (Boston: Harvard University Press, 2002).
6. http://news.bbc.co.uk/2/hi/africa/1454208.stm.

7. http://nobelprize.org/nobel_prizes/peace/laureates/1993/mandela-bio.html#.
8. John Blackstone, *CBS Evening News*, October 13, 2010.

Chapter 1: *The Leader in You*

1. http://www.whitehouse.gov/state-of-the-union-2011.
2. http://theweek.com/bullpen/column/211519/morning-in-obamas-america.

Chapter 2: *Taking Charge from Where You Are*

1. http://thinkexist.com/quotation/whenever_you_see_a_successful_business-someone/167688.html.
2. J. F. Parker, *Do the Right Thing: How Dedicated Employees Create Customers and Large Profits* (Upper Saddle River, NJ: Wharton School Publishing, 2007).
3. *Ibid.*
4. William Wordsworth, *The Complete Poetical Works* (London: Bartleby.com, 1999).

Chapter 3: *Thinking about the Future and Acting on the Present*

1. A Video Retreat™, a Paradigm Mastery Series™ with Joel Barker, Change and Leadership (St. Paul, MN: Star Thrower Distribution Corp., 1997).
2. De La Merced, Michael J. (January 2012). The New York Times .com http://dealbook.nytimes.com/2012/01/19/eastman-kodak-files-for-bankruptcy/?_php=true&_type=blogs&_r=0
3. Joyce E. Russell, Executive Leadership Strategies Program, "Understanding Your Multi-Rater Feedback Survey" (Lockheed Martin Corporation, Bethesda, July 17, 2006).
4. Viktor Frankl, *Man's Search for Meaning* (Boston: Beacon Press, 1946).
5. John H. Schaar, *Legitimacy in the Modern State* (New Brunswick: Transaction Publishers, 1981).

Chapter 4: *When Slow Is Fast and Down Is Up*

1. http://searchengineland.com/by-the-numbers-twitter-vs-facebook-vs-google-buzz-36709.

2. C. Handy, *The Elephant and the Flea: Reflections of a Reluctant Capitalist* (Boston: Harvard University Press, 2002), 101.

3. Alvin Toffler, *Future Shock* (New York: Random House, 1970).

4. Victor Godines, "Coming Soon: Basic Remote Controls Redesigned with Voice-Recognition," *The Dallas Morning News,* http://seattletimes.nwsource.com/html/businesstechnology/2009492115_pttvremote18.html.

5. John Markoff, "Smarter than You Think: Google Cars Drive Themselves in Traffic," *New York Times,* October 9, 2010, http://www.nytimes.com/2010/10/10/science/10google.html.

6. Jessica Mintz, "10 Years from Now: When iPhones will be Antiques" Pantagraph.com, December 17, 2009 http://www.pantagraph.com/news/article_235a9922-eb23-11de-995f-001cc4c03286.html.

7. John Blackstone, "Wired Teens Hooked on Electronics: Media Consumption Is a Full-Time Job for Teens, Averaging 7+ Hours on TV, Video Games, Texting, and Online," January 20, 2010, http://www.cbsnews.com/stories/2010/01/20/eveningnews/main6121496.shtml.

8. Beth J. Harpaz, "Are We Raising a Generation of Nincompoops?" *Seattle Times,* September 27, 2010.

9. Mark Bauerlein, *The Dumbest Generation* (New York: Tarcher/Penguin, 2007).

10. Randolph E. Schmid, "Study Finds People Who Multitask Often Bad at It," *Proceedings of the National Academy of Sciences* 106, no. 37 (2009), http://www.pnas.org.

11. Matt Ritchel, "Growing Up Digital, Wired for Distraction, The New York Times, November 21, 2010.

12. "Metrolink Engineer Texting with Teen Moments before Killer Commuter Crash," Fox News, September 14, 2008.

13. Saint James, Patron Saint of Spain, http://thinkexist.com/quotation/what-good-is-speed-if-the-brain-has-oozed-out-on/392011.html.

14. Sonya Eskridge, "Oprah Admits Near Meltdown" S2S Maganize. com, September 23, 2013 http://s2smagazine.com/80978/ oprah-admits-near-meltdown.

15. Matt Ritchtel, "Attached to Technology and Paying a Price," *New York Times,* June 6, 2010, http://www.nytimes. com/2010/06/07/technology/07brain.html.

Chapter 5: *The Past Is Not What It Used to Be*

1. George Santayana, *The Life of Reason: or, The Phases of Human Progress, Vol. 4* (New York: Charles Scribner's Sons, 1917).

2. D. Maraniss, *First in His Class* (New York: Simon & Schuster, 1995).

3. John H. Sheridan, "1994 Tech Leader Lew Platt: Creating a Culture for Innovation. Industry Week, December 21, 2004

4. Thomas Paine, *Common Sense, 1776* http://hua.umf.maine. edu/Reading_Revolutions/Paine.html

Chapter 6: *But That's Not Who I Am!*

1. "Full Spectrum Leadership," *Lockheed Martin Executive Leadership Handbook 2005*, 1.

Chapter 7: *Find Your Purpose, Nurture Your Passion*

1. Vincent P. Barabba, *Surviving Transformation* (New York: Oxford University Press, 2004).

2. BWW News Desk, "Young People's Chorus of NYC Celebrates Next 25 Years with Major Gala Event", http://www.ypc.org/ aboutypc/fnunez.html.

3. "Shutters 4 Scholars: Bringing Hope to the Children of Ukraine," *Business Close Up*, Maryland Public Television, 2009.

4. Omar Khayyám, translated by Edward FitzGerald, *Rubaiyat of Omar Khayyam* (Gloucester: Dodo Press, 2005).

5. Jon Bon Jovi, BrainyQuote.com, Xplore Inc, 2011, http://www. brainyquote.com/quotes/quotes/j/jonbonjovi204458.html.

Chapter 9: *Who's Painting Your Canvas?*

1. http://www.pablopicasso.org/quotes.jsp
2. M. Cassou *and S.* Cubley, *Life, Paint, and Passion: Reclaiming the Magic of Spontaneous Expression* (*New York: Tarcher Penguin, 1996*).
3. http://www.brainyquote.com/quotes/quotes/a/alfred-hitc100225.html.

Chapter 10: *Egyptian Wisdom*

1. "Job Training Brings Hope, and Work, to Middle Eastern Youth," http://www.efefoundation.org/index.php?m=5&s=2&t=9.
2. Education for Employment Foundation, http://efefoundation.org/homepage.html.

Chapter 11: *Planning Backward to Move Ahead*

1. R. L. Ackoff, *Re-Creating the Corporation* (New York: Oxford University Press, 1999).
2. http://www.searchquotes.com/quotation/The_only_way_to_predict_the_future_is_to_have_power_to_shape_the_future./21287.
3. S. Dreyfus, "Richard Bellman on the rebirth of dynamic programming", *Operations Research* INFORMS 50, no. 1, 2002, 48–51.
4. R. L. Ackoff, J. Magidson, and H. Addison, *Idealized Design: How to Dissolve Tomorrow's Crisis...Today* (Upper Saddle River, NJ: Wharton Publishing, 2006).

Chapter 12: *Leveraging Your Perspective for Enduring Change*

1. L. von Bertalanfy, *General System Theory* (Harmondsworth: Penguin, 1968).
2. W. W. Scherkenbach, *Deming's Road to Improvement* (Knoxville, TN: SPC Press, 1991).
3. *Merriam-Webster's Collegiate Dictionary,* 10th ed. (Springfield, MA: Merriam-Webster, Inc., 1998).

Chapter 13: *The Power of Design*

1. R. L. Ackoff, J. Magidson, and H. Addison, *Idealized Design: How to Dissolve Tomorrow's Crisis...Today* (Upper Saddle River, NJ: Wharton Publishing, 2006).
2. R. L. Ackoff, "A Brief Guide to Interactive Planning and Idealized Design," http://www.ida.liu.se/~steho/und/htdd01/AckoffGuidetoIdealizedRedesign.pdf.
3. *Creating the Future: An Idealized Redesign of the White House Communications Agency* (Washington, DC: White House Communications Agency, 1996).
4. J. G. Suárez, *Redesigning Systems that Work: Idealized Design in the Corridors of Power,* (Unpublished Manuscript, 2002).
5. *Building for the Twenty-First Century* (Washington, DC: The White House Communications Agency Presidential Quality Office, 1997).
6. M. L. Jacques, "Transformation and Redesign at the White House Communications Agency," interview with Dr. Gerald Suárez, *American Society for Quality Management Journal* 6, no. 3 (1999).
7. *Introduction to the White House Military Office,* CSOD Publication, (Washington, DC: The White House Military Office Customer Support and Organizational Development, 2001).

Chapter 14: *Are We There Yet?*

1. http://www.usatoday.com/sports/tennis/open/2009-08-30-usopen-federer_N.htm.
2. http://www.rogerfedererfoundation.org/en/home/

Chapter 15: *Learning to Lead and Leading to Learn*

1. R. L. Ackoff, "A Systemic View of Transformational Leadership," http://www.acasa.upenn.edu/leadership.pdf.
2. Stephen Covey, *The Leader in Me: How Schools and Parents around the World Are Inspiring Greatness, One Child at a Time* (New York: Free Press, 2008).
3. J. Wood, *Leaving Microsoft to Change the World* (New York: Harper Collins, 2006).

4. Y. Jmourko, "Inspiration for the Shutters 4 Scholars Project," unpublished essay, June 22, 2010.
5. *Ibid*
6. *Ibid*
7. http://www.unicef.org/infobycountry/ukraine_statistics.html.
8. http://www.worldorphanproject.com/statistics.html.
9. Y. Jmourko, "Inspiration for the Shutters 4 Scholars Project," unpublished essay, June 22, 2010.
10. R. Kauffman and Z. Briski, *Born into Brothels,* http://www.kids-with-cameras.org/bornintobrothels.
11. Y. Jmourko, "Inspiration for the Shutters 4 Scholars Project," unpublished essay, June 22, 2010.
12. http://www.ucareinc.org.
13. "Fifteen Years of Excellence: The Brumberger QUEST Innovation and Consulting Conference," Smith Webcast, College Park, December 2008, http://rhsmith.umd.edu/news/stories/2008/quest-conference.aspx
14. http://betweenthecolumns.umd.edu/2009/06/08/helporphans.
15. "Shutters 4 Scholars: Bringing Hope to the Children of Ukraine," *Business Close Up,* Maryland Public Television, 2009.

Chapter 16: *From Idealization to Realization: The weBike Story*

1. http://www.goodreads.com/quotes/255403-there-is-nothing-like-a-dream-to-create-the-future.
2. Aurora Pictures, *Implications Wheel*™, facilitator videos, March 1998.
3. J. Barker, *The Implications Wheel*™Video Workshop, Facilitators Guide Version 1.0 (Minneapolis, Infinity Limited, Inc., 1994).
4. Emilie Openchowski, "Bicycle-sharing program set to begin pilot this semester," http://www.diamondbackonline.com/news/bicycle-sharing-program-set-to-begin-pilot-this-semester-1.474372.
5. KabirCares, http://www.kabircares.org/citys-first-bike-sharing-program-shows-success-promise.

6. The City Fix, http://thecityfix.com/for-bikesharing-forget-stations-all-you-need-is-a-phone.

7. Kellie Woodhouse, "Pedal to the people," http://www.diamondbackonline.com/2.2795/pedal-to-the-people-1.281117.

Chapter 17: *A Leadership Imperative: Finding Your Ethical North*

1. Robert J. Stevens (speech, Center of Leadership Innovation and Change, University of Maryland, Washington, DC, October 1, 2010).

2. Stephen Covey, *The 7 Habits of Highly Effective People: Powerful Lessons in Personal Change* (New York: Fireside, 1989).

3. *Creating the Future: An Idealized Redesign of the White House Communications Agency* (Washington, DC: White House Communications Agency, 1996).

4. Senator John F. Kennedy (address, Greater Houston Ministerial Association, Rice Hotel, Houston, Texas, September 12, 1960), http://www.jfklibrary.org/Historical+Resources/Archives/Reference+Desk/Speeches/JFK/JFK+Pre-Pres/1960/Address+of+Senator+John+F.+Kennedy+to+the+Greater+Houston+Ministerial+Association.htm.

5. *Employee Handbook* (Washington, DC: White House Military Office Customer Support and Organizational Development, CSOD Publication, 2003).

6. CBS News, *60 Minutes,* interview with Katie Couric, February 8, 2009.

7. http://www.articlesbase.com/news-and-society-articles/captain-sullenberger-interview-1142149.html.

Chapter 18: *Trust Is the Glue*

1. Stephen Covey, A. R. Merrill, and R. R. Merrill, *First Things First* (New York: Simon & Schuster, 1994).

2. Douglas Martin, "Herald of Good Habits, Dies at 79" The New York Times, July, 2012.

3. http://www.nytimes.com/1989/11/25/opinion/l-what-did-columbus-know-when-did-he-know-it-481689.html.

4. http://www.brainyquote.com/quotes/quotes/t/theodorero403358.html.

Index

CPSIA information can be obtained
at www.ICGtesting.com
Printed in the USA
LVHW111020180821
695579LV00011B/87

9 781494 401368